LET US PRAY

LET US PRAY

Reformed Prayers for Christian Worship

Edited by Martha S. Gilliss

Geneva Press
Louisville, Kentucky

Scripture quotations from the New Revised Standard Version of the Bible are copyright © 1989 by the Division of Christian Education of the National Council of the Churches of Christ in the U.S.A. and are used by permission.

Book design by Sharon Adams
Cover design by Eric Walljasper, Minneapolis, MN

First edition
Published by Geneva Press
Louisville, Kentucky

This book is printed on acid-free paper that meets the American National Standards Institute Z39.48 standard. ∞

PRINTED IN THE UNITED STATES OF AMERICA

02 03 04 05 06 07 08 09 10 11 — 10 9 8 7 6 5 4 3 2 1

Library of Congress Cataloging-in-Publication Data

Let us pray : reformed prayers for Christian worship / Martha S. Gilliss, editor.—1st ed.
    p. cm.
  ISBN 0-664-50173-7 (alk. paper)
    1. Prayers. 2. Christian life—Presbyterian authors. I. Gilliss, Martha S.

  BV245 .L455 2002
  264'.051013—dc21
                                       2002072078

Contents

vi   Let Us Pray

Foreword

Why do we need yet another book of prayers? Aren't there enough already? How many books of prayers do we need? The answer to this is simple. We need new books on prayer because the human heart keeps crying out to God in an ever changing voice. While the human need for God is unchanging, how we articulate that need constantly changes. Each generation cries out to God in a new voice. To insist on offering only the prayers of ages gone by ends up turning those prayers into a false idol as we insist on making those prayers the *only* prayers.

I have always been dissatisfied with the typical prayers found in most prayer books because they never seem to speak to my situation. Instead, they speak only to the situations of ages past. As a child, I struggled with the prayers I read and heard in worship. They seemed so formal, so rigid, so passionless, and so unlike me. As a teenager, I didn't mind them so much because they gave me the opportunity to recapture a few of the minutes of sleep I had lost from staying up too late the night before. As a young adult, I developed a greater zeal for worship, but I became frustrated by the fact that my attention drifted as the prayers slowly meandered, never quite speaking to my situation and life. They were too formal. They didn't reflect the life I was living.

As a pastor, the voices of my childhood, adolescence, and young adulthood still whisper in my ear as I write my own prayers. They whisper loudly, "Don't be too formal. That's not a word I understand. Can't you say it any plainer?" It can be frustrating at times because I struggle with how to make my prayers deep yet fathomable, simple but not trivial, clear yet immersed in God's mystery, touching but not sappy, theologically sound but not long winded, grounded in tradition but not buried in the past, spiritually uplifting yet tied to real life. This is a large order and one that can be overwhelming for all of us pastors who "pray for a living."

How do we keep our prayers fresh without losing our connection to our roots? This is the challenge from age to age, generation to generation, and even year to year. Some of today's pastors err on the side of being hip, up to date, and fresh, and in the process offer prayers without soul. Many more err on the side of being so grounded in tradition that their prayers lack any kind of spiritual fire. Thus, more and more prayer books are written in an attempt to keep today and tradition in balance.

Editor Martha Gilliss has embarked on a wonderful and holy task in this book, as she has gathered prayers that achieve such a balance. These are prayers that are faithful to the Reformed tradition, yet they also speak to the real struggles of today. They do not all come from one voice but from many—from pastors who are immersed in churches large and small, old and young, rich and poor. They are eloquent yet simple, profound yet accessible, light yet filled with riches.

As you leaf through this book in search of the perfect prayers for your worship, you will find a wide variety of voices to touch you and your congregation. Where most books of prayer offer the same voice over and over again in an order that is rigid and predictable, Martha has simply placed the prayers she has collected in their appropriate season, and then has let them speak for themselves. So you will find litanies next to collects, prayers of adoration next to confessions, and poetry next to prose. And with each you will find a different and fresh voice filled with the words of the Holy Spirit, who offers to God our hearts' deepest concerns (Rom. 8:26–27).

My prayer for you is that as you use this book, it will become a resource that you will return to over and over again. I hope that as you do, the fresh winds of the Holy Spirit will blow through your congregation and community, awakening their slumbering souls and stirring them to embrace the presence of Christ as he leads them to join in praise and prayer to our Holy Creator. I hope that these prayers will contribute to the challenge at the heart of each congregation to become the body of Christ united in worship of God.

N. Graham Standish

Introduction

What does it mean to pray in worship? Is praying in this context different from praying alone? Is prayer inextricably linked to worship? We can say that while it is quite possible to pray alone or informally with others, worship without prayer cannot be real worship.

When we pray in the context of worship, our spiritual connection to those around us can become crystal clear. Our eyes and our ears and sometimes our senses of touch are opened to the presence of these others with us before God. The basic purpose of worship is to glorify and to praise God, and its order reflects its three basic functions: praise, proclamation, and presence. Communal prayer is the conscious self-presentation of God's people to the One who claims us together as beloved, and it enacts the truth that we are never truly alone before God. Prayer in this context takes on a different, and in some ways more powerful, quality as individual hearts, minds, and voices are transformed into that specific form of community known as the body of Christ.

Not that individual prayer has no role to play in the conversations with God that are our lives. Indeed, to the contrary, it is a means of receiving and responding to God's care for us and for the world, and one cannot fully participate in communal worship without the kind of intimate familiarity with God that grows stronger through the discipline of prayer at the individual level. This kind of prayer nurtures a trust in God which allows us to reach out to others and to love them as ourselves. Jesus went off by himself to pray—in the wilderness, during his ministry, and finally alone on the cross, feeling forsaken by God and abandoned by his disciples, who had followed him faithfully all the way to Jerusalem.

Jesus taught his disciples to pray. The Lord's Prayer is the model for prayers of the Reformed faith. At the same time, Jesus also taught that true prayer comes from the heart and shares with God all that we sense and feel. God is near to

1

us, much nearer than we usually imagine. Paul tells us that Christ dwells in us richly and gives us the word of faith, and that this word is quite close to us, "on our lips and in our hearts" (Rom. 10:8b). Thus, individual prayer is a natural expression of faith, which freely offers back to God a portion of the life of each believer.

Christian worship is the intentional, corporate relationship of faithful disciples to God as the body of Christ. While the Word and the sacraments are the center of Reformed worship, neither the preaching of the Word nor the celebration of the sacraments occurs apart from prayer. We pray silently, we pray aloud, we pray in song, sometimes we pray in dance. We praise, we confess, we petition and make supplications to God. We thank God.

Often we pray familiar words that our church has prayed for a long, long time. These prayers help to ground us in God as God has been known in our tradition. Like the Lord's Prayer, these prayers teach us about God as we pray the words that they speak for us. For this reason, these prayers can be comforting when we feel lost for words—and sometimes even when we feel confident and assured. Their words help us to express what is in our hearts. But sometimes these words get in the way of what we are really feeling when we pray. Sometimes our hearts are far away from the words that we utter when we pray in the context of congregational worship.

More and more, laypersons are offering the gift of their prayers on behalf of the congregation, giving their communities words to use to whisper and to shout their needs and praise to God. Pastors may or may not choose to use the prayers that are offered in the worship books of their tradition. That we need diverse words and even forms of prayer in worship is becoming apparent. God's gift of creativity is received from—and offered back to—God in manifold ways!

At the same time that our tradition encourages lay members to offer their gifts as leaders in corporate worship, it clearly does not want to relinquish all standards of decency and order! Thus, Reformed prayers retain certain qualities that set them off from some other prayers. These include:

> The aim to be theologically sound by celebrating the sovereignty of God
> and the grace that we know in Jesus Christ
> The desire for a closer understanding of God
> The free expression of all emotions, in the way of the Psalms
> A tone that is thankful and/or expectant of mercy, even if rage or discouragement is the dominant tenor.
> Intimacy
> Honesty and openness
> Acceptance that prayer itself is a gift of grace

The prayers in this book have all been written by ministers and elders from the Reformed tradition, and they all express themes common to daily life. Most of them have been written specifically for use in worship, but some have not. Some prayers are obviously recognizable as the genre that they are; others express praise, confession, seeking, thanksgiving, sorrow, or joy in poetic form. The prayer-poems may be used in services of worship, but because they function at the precognitive level of awareness, the level that is sensitive to aesthetic modes of creativity, they are especially helpful for use in meditation or as inspiration for the creation of new prayers. The hope for this book as a whole is that it will be helpful in preparing the minds and hearts of worship leaders and worshipers alike to reach out to God in the context of congregational worship.

The Reformed faith has always claimed to be the priesthood of all believers and has been grounded in the faith that Christ alone intercedes for us as we pray. These prayers are offered not so much as exemplars of creative writing as stimulants to inspire greater diversity of prayer in corporate worship. Different people and different congregations are at ease with various styles of prayer. Based on this tenet, *Let Us Pray: Reformed Prayers for Christiam Worship* offers examples of prayers to use as they are in worship, to modify as the need may be, and to use as material for reflection or as springboards for inspiration for the creation of prayers.

You will notice that the prayers have been arranged according to the liturgical calendar year. The prayers from Advent through Pentecost follow the order of worship that is shown in the *Book of Common Worship* of the Presbyterian Church (U.S.A.):[1]

> opening prayer
> call to worship
> prayer of the day or opening prayer
> adoration and praise;
> confession and assurance of pardon
> intercession and supplication
> offering dedication
> thanksgiving

Another section of the book contains prayers for special occasions in ordinary time, such as Baptism, celebration of the Lord's Supper, thanksgiving, and death.

---

1. *Book of Common Worship*, prepared by the Theology and Worship Unit for the Presbyterian Church (U.S.A.) and the Cumberland Presbyterian Church (Louisville, Ky.: Westminster/John Knox Press, 1993).

The strong assurance of faith that nothing can separate us from God's love for us in Christ binds this collection together. As the prayers in this volume voice this assurance through the common human actions of praising, yearning, confessing, hoping, repenting, grieving, thanking, and loving, they remind us that we belong to God's reign in the here and now, as God's Holy Spirit works in and through us to do God's work on earth.

Prayers for the Seasons

Advent/Christmas

Opening Prayer

Hope of history, and our hope,
    Thou so small, yet so large
    So fragile, yet so strong.
    Draw near and prepare us
    To honor what the world thinks small,
    The weak, expendable and the damned.
    Prepare for the new Jerusalem
    By way of Bethlehem, and show us the way.
                  Donna Schaper

Call to Worship

Leader: Let us rejoice on this day of joy, for Christ is coming into our lives, ready to lead us in ways of love, peace, and grace.

Congregation: So let us come to God this morning with arms outstretched and receive God's promises, blessings, and love.

N. Graham Standish

Leader: Let us sing about the loving deeds of the Lord so that we can pro-claim God's faithfulness throughout every generation.

Congregation: For God has given us the gift of Jesus Christ—the gift of God's presence among us. So let us rejoice, for Christ is about to be born in us.

N. Graham Standish

Leader: There is a birth taking place today in all people who let God's Spirit enter their lives, for in becoming open to God, we are all incarnating Christ in our hearts.

Congregation: So let us give birth to Christ's love in our hearts and lives this morning, and let us become one in Christ as we worship today.

N. Graham Standish

Leader: The world continues to languish in darkness—in the darkness of systematic and ideological evils that outdo the mere combination of our sins and those of other individuals, in the darkness of disease and natural disasters that are often not traceable to human fault, in the darkness we sometimes love better than light because we have something to hide.

People: But light has shone into the world's darkness, and the darkness has never quenched it.

Leader: There is darkness of loneliness, grief, and depression.

People: But the light shines on in the dark, and the darkness has never quenched it.

Leader: There is darkness of guilt, fear, and disappointment.

People: But the light shines on in the dark, and the darkness has never quenched it.

Leader: There is darkness of alienation, discrimination, and exploitation.

People: But the light shines on in the dark, and the darkness has never quenched it.

Leader: There is darkness of hunger, poverty, and crime.

People: But the light shines on in the dark, and the darkness has never quenched it.

Leader: There is darkness of oppression, intolerance, and ignorance.

People: But the light shines on in the dark, and the darkness has never quenched it.

Leader: There is darkness of abuse, terrorism, and torture.

People: But the light shines on in the dark, and the darkness has never quenched it.

Leader: There is darkness of apartheid, war, and possible nuclear winter.

People: But the light shines on in the dark, and the darkness has never quenched it.

Leader: There is darkness of death.

People: But the light shines on in the dark, and even the powers of death shall not prevail against it.

C. Eric Mount Jr.

First Sunday of Advent

Leader: We begin this Advent season knowing that God has created a world of many wonders. But despite God's gifts in our lives, many throughout our world suffer from unnecessary pain: hunger and starvation, prejudice and hatred, greed and injustice, violence and war. The wonders of our Creator need to be restored, and we long for the birthing of a new time, when all life's meaning and purpose will be brought to light. We long to see the shaping of God's dreams being realized in our brothers and sisters.

O God, the Master Weaver of our lives, we light this Advent candle as a simple sign of our faith in you. We pray that your light will dispel the darkness in our world, and that your light will be woven into the fabric of our lives. Let us pray together:

All: Almighty God and Creator, we are all the work of your hand. Give us the strength and faith to look to you even in our brokenness and pain. May we wait for your coming with eagerness and hope, trusting that you will renew us and all your creation; through Jesus Christ. Amen.

Gwen L. Bronson

Second Sunday of Advent

Leader: On this second Sunday of Advent, we look to the wonders of creation. Before there were mountains and mornings and meadows and birds making homes in trees, there was the mystery of God's love. This love is revealed as God weaves all good things into a cloth of great beauty. God says, "Let there be light," and there is light. When this creation must be renewed and redeemed, God says, "Prepare my way." And John the Baptist cries out in the wilderness, proclaiming love and truth, justice and peace, and the coming of God into our lives.

We light this candle as a sign of our belief in the Creator working in the tapestry of our lives. We proclaim that God is Weaver, Giver, Maker, Lover, Dreamer, and Author of all. Let us pray together:

All: Great Creator God, may we be open to the spirit of John the Baptist, who proclaimed your coming. Help us to hold fast to the promise of your creative and transforming love even when this world seems a wilderness to us. Help us to prepare your way in this world, so that your glory may be revealed and all people shall see it together; through Jesus Christ. Amen.

Gwen L. Bronson

Third Sunday of Advent

Leader: On this third Sunday of Advent, we look to the God of harmony, who holds all of us together. We praise the Weaver's golden thread that unites us all: each star and moon, each sea and stone, all wind and rain, both night and day, each sight and sound, each birth and death, both young and old, all great and small. We are all in God's hands, and as harvest follows seedtime, so God's love for us comes to fullness.

We light this candle as a sign of hope that the harmony of God's world may be revealed to us. We wait to see the true light of the world. Let us pray together:

All: God of harmony and light, help us to see your loving plan for our lives. Comfort those of us who mourn. Give us patience and courage to wait for your harvest, when what we have sown in tears we will reap with joy. Give us the vision to see your presence in our lives. You have done great things for us—open our hearts to know your goodness. Amen.

Gwen L. Bronson

Fourth Sunday of Advent

Leader: On this fourth Sunday of Advent, we look to the steadfast God who has made an everlasting covenant with us. We look for the One who has come to give love a name and who is love, the One who has come to show us the way and who is the way. We look for the One whose life will never cease, whom death cannot contain; we look for the One who weaves joy out of sadness.

We light this candle as a sign of our trust in God's covenant in human form, forging a bond between us so strong that not even death can break it.

All: Let us pray: Eternal and all-powerful God, we thank you for the covenant of love that binds us together. Even when we lose hope and turn away from you, you reach out to us; you make whole our brokenness. Even from the fragments of our lives, you weave a tapestry of great beauty. Nothing is impossible with you. You have prepared a place for us—let us not rest until we find our way home and rest in you. Amen.

Gwen L. Bronson

Christmas Eve

Leader: On this Christmas Eve, we give thanks for God's holy design in our lives. God's very presence surprises and sustains us when we least expect it, ever since a child was wrapped in bands of cloth and laid in a manger in Bethlehem. With all creation we raise our voices in praise and sing a new song: Glory to God in the highest and peace and goodwill to all people on earth.

We light this candle in gratitude for the design God weaves in our lives. We are meant for communion, and God brings us together by the great gift of love we celebrate tonight. Let us pray together:

All: Merciful and loving God, we thank you for the gift of your love and presence, brought home to us in the birth of Jesus. We can only marvel as we come before you in humility and awe. Help us to reach out to others as you have reached out to us. May those of us who are poor and homeless experience your loving presence as surely as Mary and Joseph did, and may all of us come to know that we have no home except in you. Amen.

Gwen L. Bronson

Adoration

As the birth of any child is a miracle beyond our comprehension, O God, how much more so is the birth of Mary's child. We cry out in awe and wonder at the marvel of your love and the mystery of your Word made flesh. May we, through all our days, bring honor to our Lord, who shared life in the flesh with us. In Christ's holy name we pray. Amen.

Mark H. Landfried

Praise

Clouds nod as they pass
    Stars shine with brilliance
Within the cosmos there is heard
    A great chorus
Angels having special solos
    The fabric of life taking on new texture
Smiles come more easily
    Hands reach out less hesitantly to strangers
Lions and calves walk peacefully together
    Hungry are fed
Lame walk
    A special star shown with great brilliance
To lead the way
    And it came to pass
It was Christmas.

Raymond Hearn

Confession

There is a deep hunger within us, O Christ, for the food only you can give us: the bread of life found in you. We need you so desperately in our lives, and only you can satisfy our deep hunger. Yet we are such an impatient people. We want to be fed by you, but we don't always want to sit at your table. We want fast spiritual food, not the nourishing food that comes through patient prayer, quiet reflection, service, thanksgiving, understanding, and virtue. We want your saving grace to work in a hurry so we can experience your blessings and peace now. We are not always willing to undergo the slow transformation that allows you to enter our very souls. Help us to come to you with repentant hearts so that in your grace we can become your disciples, your servants, and your apostles. In Christ's name we pray. Amen.

N. Graham Standish

Assurance of Pardon

The way to Christ is simple but hard. It requires repentant hearts—hearts that are willing to turn away from sin and toward God's grace. Our sin can be so deep that we don't even sense it working in our lives, but when we give our lives to Christ, our sin is slowly but surely wiped away so that the light of God shines from our hearts. Christ came not to judge us but to heal us down to our souls so that our lives can be made whole.

N. Graham Standish

Holy Lord, you call on us to live lives of quiet faith, ready to trust you and your word for us. You tell us to follow Christ and, like Jesus, to let your Spirit be incarnated within each of us, so that we can become little Christs in the world. Yet we hesitate. There is so much we don't understand, and we let this weaken our faith. We keep thinking that we can understand and figure out all your mysteries, but this is not the way of faith. The way of faith and the way of Christ is to follow you and trust in you despite our uncertainties. You ask us simply to have faith, to let your Spirit live in our hearts, and to live the life of Christ. Help us to form this kind of faith. In Christ's name we pray. Amen

N. Graham Standish

Assurance of Pardon

We have been offered the way of true freedom, and it comes through faith. Whenever we choose to follow Christ and to live as God calls us, all sorts of possibilities emerge in our lives. We discover new and deeper ways to live, love, and serve. It is in letting the Spirit of Christ be incarnated within us that God's grace becomes most powerful in our world.

N. Graham Standish.

Heavenly Father, who in Jesus Christ comes to rule the world with truth and grace, we confess that we have gone astray, all of us to our own ways. The ways we have chosen for ourselves have led us into a dark wood where thorns of selfishness abound and where we seem only to hurt ourselves and others. Forgive us our sins, and send that one who makes a path out of the wilderness, a highway for our God, even Jesus Christ. Prepare our hearts to receive him so that his blessing might flow far as the curse is found. We pray in Christ's name. Amen.

Thomas W. Currie III

Leader: It is Advent. It is the season in which we prepare our hearts to welcome Christ, who is the bringer of all peace. We confess to you the ways in which we block the peace of Christ in our lives.

People: God of peace, hear our prayer.

Leader: The rushing and scurrying to get things done,

People: We confess to you, O God of peace.

Leader: The worry about the little details,

People: We confess to you, O God of peace.

Leader: The financial burdens we put on ourselves,

People: We confess to you, O God of peace.

Leader: The impatience and irritability we feel and take out on one another,

People: We confess to you, O God of peace.

Leader: The bickering and quarreling we get into because we are too busy,

People: We confess to you, O God of peace.

Leader: Though we make ourselves less than peaceful at this time of the year, your peace is always there for us.

People: Instill within us your peace, O God.

Leader: When we feel overwhelmed,

People: Instill within us your peace, O God.

Leader: When we are filled with worry,

People: Instill within us your peace, O God.

Leader: When we become irritable,

People: Instill within us your peace, O God.

Leader: When the guilt of our ways threatens to overcome us, help us to remember that we are forgiven in Christ.

People: Instill within us your peace, O God.

Leader: Instill within us your peace, O God. Instill within us your peace, and help us to make choices that bring us closer to you. Help us to be more peaceful so that we may spread Christ's peace and love to others. Amen.

Susan R. Tomlinson

O Holy Lord of hope, in this season of holy anticipation, hear us as we come to you with humble hearts. You created us to feel the deep joy of your presence and to share in the wonders of your love. You created us to be people of prayer, to be people who discover you in prayer and grow deeper in our love of you through prayer. You created us to be people of awe and wonder who look around our lives and discover your presence everywhere, bringing light and life to everything. You created us to be all of these, yet we can become so wrapped up in the struggles of life that we shut out you and your joy. We can become so busy that we never pray, let alone discover you in prayer. We can become so focused on this and that that we never look up from our lives to discover your mystery all around us. Touch our hearts this morning so that we can become people of joy, prayer, and gratitude who shine with your presence. In Christ's name we pray. Amen.

N. Graham Standish

Assurance of Pardon

If you are willing to open up to God, you will discover God's grace and blessings all around you. Paul said, "Rejoice always, pray without ceasing, give thanks in all circumstances." When we do this, we discover just how powerful and present God is. This is the God Christ revealed, a God who is with us, around us, above us, beyond us, behind us, and before us. This is the God of Christ who loves us so deeply that no sin is so great or act so horrible that we cannot be embraced in love.

N. Graham Standish

Intercession and Supplication

Take us to Bethlehem, O God, where your heart of love was revealed in Mary's child. But keep us, we pray, from lingering too long at the manger, as though the story ended there. Take us to Calvary, where love triumphed over hate, and take us to Easter's empty tomb, where life triumphed over death, for it is in the powerful love and loving power of our risen Lord that we find strength for the living of our days. Amen.

Mark H. Landfried

We have been blessed, O God, by the stories passed on to us of those days when the world was holding its breath in anticipation of the coming of the Christ, then of that day when, in a burst of marvel, its greatest hopes and dreams were fulfilled. Thrill us again with the stories of the babe of Bethlehem, and show us how to tell our own stories of what his coming has meant to us, so

that others through our witness will know the power of his redeeming love.
Amen.

Mark H. Landfried

God, keep us alert for the signs of the gentle touch of your hand upon your
world. Whether it be a star in the sky or a voice in the night, help us to have
the courage to follow where you will lead, and to rely on your guiding presence along the way. Be with us and use us to give honor to your Son as we
witness to his love; for it is in his name that we pray. Amen.

Mark H. Landfried

Keep us, O God, from being so caught up in the beautiful sounds of Christmas that we fail to hear in the distance the ugly sounds of Golgotha. Show
us again the horror of the sins of our lives that led our Lord to that place of
his broken and bleeding heart, but show us also the power of his love revealed
in the cradle and cross. It is in that love that we pray. Amen.

Mark H. Landfried

Eternal God—for whom all people wait and search, even when they don't
realize it, whose voice is heard in recordings by prophets and saints of old
and by your faithful people in our own time—we cry out today for a live
and present word from you. As our season of discontent approaches the day
of your coming, we pray that you would speak to us in the graceful ways
that you know best.

Open our eyes that have been closed by fear and blinded by self-pity, that
we may see you even in the anxieties and uncertainties that beset our days
and threaten to overwhelm us like a cloud of darkness.

Help us to see that, amid the hustle and bustle of this holiday time—the
crowded stores and rude shoppers, the impatient drivers, the frayed
nerves—you have become incarnate, sanctifying the smallest tasks of love,
generosity, and kindness that we are enabled by your grace to perform.

We think of the needs of others at this time, O Lord, and we are embar-
rassed by our selfishness. May the answer to our prayers begin with us to
redeem the times. Bring to all those who are in need the alleviation of their
poverty, or comfort for their minds and spirits. Enable us to do what we can
to help them—to share our own happiness and prosperity, to provide a listening ear or friendly word, to do errands or acts of kindness. But let us not
be content so long as conditions exist that foster human distress from generation to generation through the repetition of ignorance, filth, and disease.

We pray that the promise of your birth—that peace shall be on earth—may soon be fulfilled, both in our troubled hearts and in our troubled world. Come to us, Lord, for we need your presence in our own lives. We pray especially for those dear to us who are sick, or troubled, or unsure, or who are near the hour of their death. Comfort, comfort your people, and fill each heart with your love.

We pray for the world into which you came and which you still love. Touch us anew with the hope that is the heritage of those who love you and trust your promises.

Through Jesus Christ, who is the joy of those who are happy and the comfort of those who mourn, as we join the church in the family prayer: Our Father . . .

John T. Ames

Eternal God, we do not pray that you will come and be among us, for we know that you are already with us. We ask, rather, that you will open our eyes to your presence, that we will see you at work in us, in our neighbors, in our church, and in the world, which you made and which you continue to love.

In this season of anticipation, we pray that we might not only be mindful that you came to women and men in times past in the person of Jesus of Nazareth, but that we might be sensitive to your coming to us in the here and now of our lives. Give us also the hope that in the future your promise will be perfected, that your glory might be revealed to all flesh and that your will shall be done on earth.

We are thankful that you come to us—in our history, in our present—and we hope for the future fulfillment of your kingdom.

Surely, O God, it is you who saves us. We will trust in you and not be afraid.

We pray your blessings as well on your world—the world into which you came and into which we are sent as your body. We pray especially for the world's victims—in [*name places where there is war and violence*], in the hills and hollows of this state, and in the alleys and housing projects of this city. Be with those who suffer.

Be also with those who need you in the comfortable homes and spacious lawns of our own pleasant community, for sometimes we suffer too. We pray for those who are lonely—who have no family or friends for whom to buy gifts. We pray for those whose family circle is broken in the holiday time, for those who are sick, for those who are worried about children, or spouses, or jobs, or money, for those who feel themselves without a purpose in the world.

We pray for your church—waiting in hopeful expectation, gathered in worship, dispersed in service to your people.

We pray for this community, locked in the frenzy of holiday preparations. Help us to get the Christmas spirit without being overcome by the busy-ness we impose upon it. Help us to remember—even in [*name a local shopping center*]—that this is a time of joy and peace and tranquility. Help us to keep things in perspective and not to get carried away by trivia.

Help us always to remember what it is we are doing, what we are celebrating, and in whose name we give gifts. Be with us and save us; through Jesus Christ our Lord, who taught us to pray: Our Father . . .

John T. Ames

As we continue to await the great festival of Christmas, let us prepare ourselves so that we may be shown its true meaning.

Let us hear, in the lessons of Holy Scripture, how the prophets of Israel foretold that God would visit and redeem God's waiting people.

Let us rejoice, in our carols and hymns, that the good purpose of God is being mightily fulfilled among us.

Let us celebrate the promise that our Lord and Savior will bring all peoples and nations into the glory of God's eternal kingdom, in which the blind will receive their sight, the lame will walk, the lepers will be healed, the deaf will hear, and the poor will receive good news. And let us await with confident hope the time when the earth shall be filled with the glory of God, as far as the waters cover the sea.

But first, let us pray:

> For the world that God loved and continues to love, and into which Christ came;
>
> For our own community, and for the activities that occupy our attention and to which we devote our energies;
>
> For the poor of this community, that they might be blessed by the one whose first and primary identification was with the poor; and for the children who know neither Jesus nor Santa Claus but only deprivation, violence, and hopelessness;
>
> For those who have not heard the good news, or who cannot believe it;
>
> For the church in this place and everywhere, that it might be freed from evil and fear, and may in pure joy lift up the light of the love of God;
>
> For the homes and families of this congregation, and for those in our families whom we name silently;
>
> For the sick, especially [*names*], and for those approaching the end of their life, that they might be healed in whatever way is in accordance with your will for them.

All our prayers and praises we offer to God, whom we know through Jesus Christ, as we pray in the words that Jesus Christ himself taught us: Our Father . . .

John T. Ames

O God, the flame in our darkness, we have sung the carols until we could do them in our sleep. We have spread season's greetings and gifts so widely by voice, pen, and package that we feel spent in more ways than one. We have perhaps mustered our hopes once again for a more benevolent and peaceful world, but we confess that our reservations have been as great as our expectations because we believe more in human frailty and depravity than in your power made perfect in the weakness of a stabled and tortured Jesus. Visit us now in the stillness after the noise. Enable us to respond to the angelic tidings gladly, to give ourselves beyond the demands of duty and the outward observance of expected gestures, and to get our hopes up in ways that can give new life to our existence in the new year. We pray in the name of him whose coming has made people rejoice, whose self-giving has moved people to love, whose humble power has given people reason to hope by making all things new, and who invited and taught his followers to pray: Our Father . . .

C. Eric Mount Jr.

We remember, O God, those for whom talk of the Prince of Peace sounds hollow because they are caught up in military conflict or ethnic strife, buffeted by political conflict, tormented by religious conflict, torn by interpersonal conflict, or tortured by inner conflict; those for whom the singing of "Silent Night" recalls the silence of loneliness and not that of wonder; those for whom the strains of "Joy to the World" only remind them of their sorrow over lost loved ones, lost capacities, lost health, lost usefulness, or lost hope; those for whom the flow of money during this season only makes their poverty more obvious and more frustrating; those for whom the handouts of this season only make going without the rest of the year more painful; those for whom the reunions of the season only heighten their separation from loved ones due to distance, imprisonment, hospitalization, or being held hostage; those for whom the gatherings of families and friends during the season only confirm or worsen the alienation they feel from family members and former friends. Save us from weak resignation to all of the conditions that blight the festivals for others or ourselves; through Jesus Christ our Lord, whose coming can make all things new. Amen.

C. Eric Mount Jr.

God, we give you thanks for the wonder and mystery, the lights and wrappings, the glorious "hallelujahs" and stunning "silent nights" of this season. Most of all, we give you thanks for this miracle that you have come to be with us, come to be like us, come to know us so that we might know and be with you. We pray that our spirits may be renewed and our hearts enlivened to welcome this good news—to welcome you—into our lives and into our world. May we see you in new places, hear you in new voices, work with you in new commitments to bring your peace and justice and love on earth.

We give thanks for . . .

We pray for . . .

We bring before you the places in our lives and in our world where the glorious word of your arrival has not been sounded—where the Herods still rule with terror, where the nights are still lonely, where the days are filled with white noise. God, transform our lives so that you may use us as instruments of your peace. We pray in the name of the One who is our peace. Amen.

Ann J. Deibert

God, it is Christmas—a time of great rejoicing. But sometimes we don't feel so joyful. Amidst the activities of the season we find memories of people we love who have died. Sometimes the pain of their loss is intense, and we are filled with great sadness. Help us in those times to turn to you as our source of strength. Help us to be consoled by your compassion and love. Help us to find hope in the gift of Christ and in the knowledge of eternal life in him.

We also pray for people who are facing Christmas without someone they love. Help them gently through the moments of loneliness. Be for them a source of peace. Help them to lean on you for their strength. Help them and all of us to remember your promise that nothing can ever separate us from your love in Christ. We pray in his lovely name. Amen.

Susan R. Tomlinson

Christmas Eve

All light their candles

> **Leader:** O Lord, you have given us Jesus, who is the light of the world.
>
> **People:** Help us to bring the light of Christ to a weary world.
>
> **Leader:** Where people are lost in sin,
>
> **People:** Help us to bring the light of Christ.

Leader: Where there is despair and hopelessness, where there is sadness and grief,

People: Help us to bring the light of Christ.

Leader: Where there is sickness and suffering, where there is violence,
hatred, prejudice, cruelty, and domination,

People: Help us to bring the light of Christ.

Leader: O Lord, so fill us with your love, your peace, and your goodness that doubt and mistrust may be dispelled within us and we
may be Christ's light in a world of strife.

All: Amen.

Susan R. Tomlinson

Offering Dedication

Gracious God, you have shown your great love for your children by using
commonplace things for your purpose—water to mark your children, bread
and wine to feed and nurture us ordinary people to be disciples, a child in a
manger to announce your grace. Take these commonplace things, these gifts
of paper and metal and the lives that stand behind them. Bless and use them
to proclaim your gracious love, for we offer them in the name of Jesus, the
Lamb of God. Amen.

Mary Marple Thies

Thanksgiving

O God, whose name is Love, we thank you that in your beloved Son you
shared human life with us, knowing birth from a mother's womb at its beginning and the passage through the valley of the shadow of death at its ending. Cradle us in your arms and hold us in your loving care, that we may
also know that life without end, where every tear will be wiped away and
where mourning and crying and pain will be no more. Amen.

Mark H. Landfried

First Sunday after Christmas

Intercession

Out of the noise and glitter and excitement of the Christmas frenzy, we have come away, O God, into this hour in your presence. Help us to discover here the meaning and joy that lie beneath the surface of the holy day. Help us to see beyond the story of a baby in a manger and realize the truth of Christmas—that you come to us in Jesus, that you live with us, sharing our joys and sorrows, redeeming every act of love and forgiving every act of hate for which we repent. Enable us to test our lives by the standard of God incarnate, judging ourselves by Christ's teaching and example. Then send us out to spread the word that you are born among us and that you live with us.

Living God, moved by the coming of Christ into our lives, we seek to be your people. Help us to live in faithful covenant with you and with one another. Let the peace of Christ be our guide, and let Christ's message in all its richness live in our hearts.

Amazing God, you have confounded the wisdom of the world by coming to us in the form of a human baby, frail and vulnerable. Help us to comprehend the great love with which you have opened yourself to us and to our world, that we in turn may risk opening ourselves in love toward all your people.

God of compassion, we pray for all those who do not share our Christmas joy—for those who are lonely, for whom holiday times bring additional sadness and more loneliness;

> For those who suffer from the cold due to inadequate clothing shelter and fuel;

> For the children in our community who know neither Jesus nor Santa Claus, for whom Christmas is like every other day, filled with deprivation and neglect;

For the children who know too much Santa Claus, who know only the joy of receiving and who learn that they deserve to have whatever they want.

We pray also for the world into which Christ came, the world you love so much. We pray in the hope that the promise of the angels of peace on earth may be fulfilled—and that we might be given the grace to participate in its fulfillment.

Blessed be the Lord God of Israel, for God has visited and redeemed his people. Hear our prayers, O Lord, as we join in your church's favorite prayer: Our Father . . .

John T. Ames

New Year

Intercession

Eternal God, a thousand years in your sight are but as yesterday. They pass as quickly as one night's watch.

Whatever the significance of this new century, yesterday morning was the same as the dawning of every day since you first created life and light and proclaimed it all "very good."

We acknowledge your lordship over the world that you have made and over the creatures that you have placed in it. We acknowledge your lordship over us—feeble creatures who vainly strive to be masters of the universe that you made and over which you still rule.

We are very impressed with our technology—indeed, it is very impressive—but our inventions are made with the brains and the skills and the knowledge and zeal that you impart.

As we move further into this new century, we affirm with confidence your lordship in the future, based on our conviction that you have been Lord from the beginning. We are sure of nothing as we face the future, except that you remain Lord of the world that you created and that you still love.

You have filled us with the light of your word, made flesh in Jesus Christ. Let the light of faith shine in all that we do, that the one who is from everlasting to everlasting—yet who was born among us and lived with us—may continue to inspire the thoughts of our hearts and the actions of our lives.

As you have led us in days past, so guide us now and always, that our hearts may learn to choose your will and new resolves be strengthened.

Help us to face the future with confidence, knowing that you have guided and led your people through the eons past, and knowing also that you are a personal God, concerned not just with the mighty forces of wind and weather and of the destiny and fate of nations but also with the joys and sorrows that characterize our lives.

You have filled us with the light of your Word, made flesh in Jesus Christ. Let the light of faith shine in all that we do, that the one who is from ever-lasting to everlasting—yet who was born among us and lived with us— may continue to inspire the thoughts of our hearts and the actions of our lives.

Bless especially this day those who are in need: the people we do not know, whose hope for the future is not buoyed by the experience of bless-ing in the past, who have not known healing, or faith, or prosperity, and who have no hope.

Bless also those known to us who need to sense your healing presence today—especially [names], and others whom we name silently.

You have been our God in ages past, and we know that you will continue to be our God in years to come. And so wrap us in your arms of love, as together at the beginning of this new day, this new year, this new century, we join in the church's ancient prayer: Our Father . . .

John T. Ames

Great God, in voicing our intercessions, we acknowledge that the needs we mention are often ours as well as those of others, and we ask not that you fix everything and spare us from responsibility, but that you shape us so that we may be means of grace to others for whom we pray. We pray now

> For those who anticipate death by evading life because they fear the transforming death of self-loss and change, and for those who spend life fleeing death or being obsessed with fighting it because they fear its power more than they believe in yours;
>
> For those too careful to care for anyone, and for those so uncared for that they suspect and withhold care;
>
> For those too defensive about assuring their status to face criticism, and for those so unsure of themselves that they can only maintain their status by dispensing criticism;
>
> For those too anxious about their security to be productive, and for those too complacent in their security to be productive;
>
> For those whose vision of the public good has been blurred by their visions of personal glory and gain, and for those whose impoverished vision and powerless position make them unable to contribute to the pub-lic good;
>
> For the half of the world that is hungry or malnourished, and for the other half that has help to give if it has the will to give it and the sense to avoid making it a means of control;

For those who labor to provide medical care for all, and for those who struggle without the medical care they need or under the crushing financial burden of medical care they have gotten;

For those who seek to promote the liberation of people, and for those whose bodies and minds are twisted and tortured by human inhumanity, and for those who do the twisting and torturing;

For those who seek to establish equal justice under the law, and for those who have been used badly by the law or who have used the law badly in their own interests;

For the powers that be, that they may have an ear for the powerless, and for antagonists in conflict, that they may become partners in peace.

O maker of all things new, make us and our world new so that a new year may not simply bring more of the same. These our prayers we offer in the name of Jesus Christ our Lord. Amen.

C. Eric Mount Jr.

Epiphany

Call to Worship

Leader: Arise, for our light has come and the glory of God has risen upon us. The shadows of the world have been dispersed through God's gift of Jesus.

Congregation: Let us rejoice and lift up our eyes to see God's light as it dwells in us, filling us with faith, hope, and love.

N. Graham Standish

Confession

Holy God, your presence in Christ truly was and remains an epiphany. Your people were immersed in the darkness of oppression and despair, yet you came through Christ to reveal not only your love but your presence. You showed us that you are with us no matter what may befall. Through Christ, you taught us that the way to discover you is through faith, hope, and love. You showed us that through faith we can be healed, renewed, and filled with your Spirit. Too often we close our eyes to your epiphany and remain in darkness. Help us to open our eyes and our hearts to you so that we can discover Christ's love growing in our souls. In Christ's name we pray. Amen.

N. Graham Standish

Assurance of Pardon

The light of God surrounds us, and all it takes is open eyes to see it. When we walk in faith, we discover God's light brightening even the darkest corners of our lives. This is the way of Jesus, who in the darkest moments of his life said to God, "Not my will, but thy will be done." When we live life with this kind of faith, we discover in the end that God has been working wonders all around us. Friends, believe the good news of the gospel. Amen.

N. Graham Standish

Intercession

Work your miracle of life within us, O God. Lift us out of our darkness and show us the light that has come into the world through your beloved Son. Bring joy to our hearts and grant us the transforming power of your presence; through Jesus Christ our Lord. Amen.

Mark H. Landfried

Midwinter

Intercession

Gracious God, in a week in which we have been glued to the Weather Channel, we pause to acknowledge your lordship over the world that you have made. Whether we enjoy or curse the snow and the cold, every season reminds us that you are a God of all seasons, that your world is governed by immutable laws of wind and tide that you established and that always work. Give us a sense of humility as we confront the fact that we cannot control—even if we can predict—the vagaries of nature that affect our lives so inescapably in the winter.

We ask your forgiveness for the sins we have committed against your world: for polluting the atmosphere with carbon dioxide from the machines that we think are essential for our lives, ignoring the fact that if the air disappears, or if the sea rises a foot, it won't matter what kind of transportation system we used to have.

On this day, remind us that you have not left yourself without witnesses in any age. Wherever people have walked this earth, you have taken up residence among them and have revealed yourself to them. You were present with Abraham in Mesopotamia, with Paul in his Roman prison, with the leaders of our history, and with the founders of our congregation. And you are present with us, to whom the promise is given: On this rock I will build my church, and the gates of hell shall not prevail.

During these many years, this church has witnessed to your presence and grace in this community. Speak to us as you spoke to those who have gone before us. Fill us with your grace that sustained them. Give us the zeal to build upon the foundations they laid and to fulfill the promises they strove to obey.

Remind us once again of the grace of our Lord Jesus Christ, by which we are saved from meaninglessness and frustration and selfishness and hell. Rekindle in us the joy we experienced when we first accepted your invitation to join you in covenant. And let us go forth, rekindled and renewed, to enlarge the circle of your covenant people.

We pray today for your benediction upon all who are particularly in need. We pray for those in our congregation and in our families who are sick, while we give you gratitude and thanks for your healing mercies in the lives of [names]. We pray also for those who are lonely, for those in distress, for those we love the most.

And we pray also, as we always do, the church's family prayer: Our Father . . .

John T. Ames

Lent

Praise

We praise you, O God, for the compassionate love we have seen in our Lord: that love that will not give up on us even when we do nothing except boast about our loyalty and then run away when the going gets rough; that love that forgives us and calls us to new life in your presence. Thank you, God. In Christ's name we pray. Amen.

Mark H. Landfried

Confession

Holy God, we thank you for this Lenten season. It is a much needed time for us to concentrate more fully on strengthening our relationship with you. We confess the lack of zeal with which we often approach this relationship. We confess the times when our love of the activities of this world overrides our love of spending time with you. We confess the ways we shut you out of our lives. Help us to resolve anew to grow in our desire to be close to you, for the sake of Christ's work on earth. Amen.

Susan R. Tomlinson.

Supplication

Show us again, O God, the compassionate love of our Lord, who suffered for our sins, who took our humiliation upon himself and died on the cross to make us whole, who runs to meet us on the road, throws his arms around us, and welcomes us home. In his love we pray. Amen.

Mark H. Landfried

Help us, O God, to recognize what may be our Judas ways: our impatience when things are not working out as we think they should, and our failure to remember vows of loyalty made and gifts of love received. Shock us with the potential for betrayal residing within us, and strengthen us for faithful service; through Jesus Christ our Lord. Amen.

Mark H. Landfried

God of the ages and giver of all good things, we rejoice in your greatest gift: the Child of Bethlehem, Man of Galilee, Suffering Savior on Calvary's cross, King of kings and Lord of lords in the garden of the Easter dawn. As we respond to his wonderful love and amazing grace, make us faithful in our discipleship and bold in our witness, that we may find new life in him and serve him all our days. Amen.

Mark H. Landfried

Work your miracle of life within our lives, O God, we pray. Touch us in your mercy, that in our weakness we may know your love. Lift us out of the darkness of our despair into that place of hope where the dawn is breaking and life starts fresh and new; through Jesus Christ our Lord, risen from the dead and alive forever more. Amen.

Mark H. Landfried

Intercession

Eternal God, you feed the hungry and satisfy the thirsty. You befriend the lonely, travel with those who are desperate, comfort those who mourn. We have no needs that you cannot meet. You lift us when we are depressed, and your power humbles us when we are proud. Your courage strengthens us when we are afraid, and your peace calms us when we are embattled.

Your faithfulness is no accident, and our faith in you is not born of chance. We test you at every turn. We bargain with you, tempt you, abandon you, blame you. Yet you continue to be our God. Your patience is a match for your faithfulness. You understand the pain that drives us to despair—the child who goes another way, the parent who will not let a child grow up, the spouse who rejects us, the friend who drinks to ruin, the partner who dies. You know us, you understand us, you love us.

Your love for us is demonstrated in that while we were yet sinners—while we were totally unworthy of your love—you loved us. And you demonstrated that love in the most vivid way possible.

We thank you for love, and we pray for a greater capacity to love. We thank you for the love between a man and a woman, for the love that parents have for their children and that children have for their parents. We thank you also for friendship, for loving relations with all sorts of people, for hugs and embraces, for smiles and laughter, for shared sorrow and tears.

Give us a greater sense of beauty—the beauty of a spring morn—of the first tiny glimpses of purple and yellow in our flower beds, of children playing, of two lives grown old together.

Bless your church today as it continues to struggle to make ancient truth relevant to new times and new problems. Especially we pray your blessing upon [*names of neighboring congregations and/or denominations*].

We pray also for those to whom we are the closest, whose burdens we bear the most obviously; for members of our families and of the family of this congregation who are sick, especially for [*names*]. Keep us as a family of worship and service in the name of the One who calls us to follow him: Jesus Christ our Lord, who bids us join in the church's family prayer: Our Father . . .

John T. Ames

Palm/Passion Sunday

Call to Worship

Leader: Hosanna! Hosanna! Hosanna!

People: Blessed is the one who comes in the name of the Lord!

Leader: Blessed is the coming kingdom of our ancestor David!

People: Hosanna in the highest heaven!

Leader: Let us shout praises to our Lord,

People: Spread palm branches before him,

Leader: And worship him this day and every day.

Thomas Vandergriff

Confession

Glorious God, today is a wonderful day. We love to shout "Hosanna" and wave palm branches. We confess that there are times when we lift our voices in praise of you and then turn around and speak cruelly to another. We joyfully tell you how amazing you are and then use our tongues to speak ill of another. We lift our arms gratefully to wave palm branches and then lift our voices to hurt another. Your Word tells us this is wrong, O God. Forgive us and help us to live our praise by treating others with your love and compassion. We pray for the sake of Christ's present and coming kingdom. Amen.

Susan R. Tomlinson

Intercession and Supplication

O God of mystery,
    witness to our laughter and our joy,
        our moments of triumph and clarity,
            as well as our silences, our betrayals,
            our confusion, and our violence,
who are we who could be so loved?
And who are You who dares to create and sustain the drama
        we call life and death?

We pause this morning as we enter a week we understand to be "holy,"
    a week that, as we trace the steps of the fully human One,
        captures the extremes of our lives
        and offers glimpses through the cracks
            into the mystery of our all-too-human relationship with You.

At one moment we stand waving palms,
    saying "Yes!" to You, to our lives,
        and to the wheels of history turning in our favor.
We are captured by some ineffable sense of You:
        in the smile of a child,
        the bursting into bloom of a dogwood,
        a flock of birds swooping in the sky,
        in the quiet look of an older friend,
        in campesinos who say "No!" to a withering foreign debt, or
        in peoples who say, "We will not be moved. . . .
            Keep your eyes on the prize!"
In those moments, we are given to sense You and to know the Christ
        alive
        present
        loving and
        true.

But in the blink of an eye,
    in the cascading of one mood to the next,
    another turn of the wheel, and
        the portal closes
            and we resume the futilities of our egocentrism and mistrust. . . .
In the next instant
    it is as if we lost our way.
        We are not sure what matters.
        We become consumed by us.

We turn our back on another.
We think and say we are capable of love,
    yet find ourselves unable or even unwilling
    to do precisely that which we said we could: love.
We shout, "Hosanna!" one day
    and yell, "Crucify!" the next.
We lay down palms one day
    and lie low the next.
And this is our Holy Week.

Yet in the midst of all this there is a figure:
    one who is human and is of God,
    moving through this sea of chaos and manipulations
      faithful,
      obedient to some deeper call,
      finding ways to trust
        in the love and the mercy and the compassion,
        the justice *and* the mystery
          that is You and Yours.

They were not easy days with easy answers.
Nor are they now.

Yet in the midst of this holy week
    we are given to see and sense
      some ultimate mystery:
        that you, O God, are present in it all
        through life and through death,
        bursting through our shortsightedness and limited imaginations,
        quiet beneath the noise of our circus.

Help each of us,
    our families and communities,
    our congregation,
    the Church,
    and our world,
to find such a trust and obedience in You.

You, who runs deeper than our greatest failings,
You, who flows stronger than our most hard-hearted guilt,
You, who blows fresher than our stalest sin,
You, who is present before us and with us
    here on this earth or beyond,

to You we now and always pray
in the name of the Christ,
the living mystery of Your presence. Amen.
Philip Lloyd-Sidle

Intercession

Eternal God, mysterious beyond our understanding, yet who appears in the parades of life and in the city crowds where issues are drawn and truth is trampled, hear our prayer.

We confess that we are prone to fickleness, alternating between cheering and crucifying in a vain attempt to justify ourselves. May the drama we celebrate in this Holy Week come home to us with saving power.

As people of old bowed down and sang praises and shouted "Hosanna" to your son, Jesus, we too praise him and bow down to him. We like to think that if we had been there we would have treated him with the respect he deserved, that we would have found majesty in lowliness, greatness in meekness, strength in nonviolence, truth in service, and glory in sacrifice. We like to think that instead of a crucifixion, there would have been a coronation later that week. But deep inside our souls, we know that the result would have been the same—only the names of the actors would have been different.

So this Holy Week, as we remember that Christ took upon himself the sins of the whole world, we pray that we might be given the grace to accept the suffering and burden of our sisters and brothers around the world as our own.

The Lord looked at the city and wept. So we pray for the nations and the neighborhoods in which we live. We pray in hopeful expectation for [*name an international conflict*] to be resolved peacefully. We pray for the wretchedly poor nations of the two-thirds world, where political ideology is an unaffordable luxury and where the only need is supper and a bed.

As the people of the world come more to understand the need to protect the world itself, we pray for the air and the water and the land that you created and that you call "good." As we struggle with the dilemma caused by the necessity to protect the environment and the desire to protect investments, we pray for the world.

We also pray for your church, as we join with millions of brothers and sisters in this Holy Week. We pray for this congregation that we love and for the denomination of which we are a proud part. We pray also for all who bear the name of Christ—by whatever other name they are also known. Especially today we pray for [*name particular groups or organizations*].

Enable us to recognize you, alive and active in the world, in your church, and in the lives of the women and men who serve you. Come to us now by the familiar path by which your grace is known to us. Minister to our hidden needs and answer our silent prayers.

Hear us as we join together in the prayer your son gave his church: Our Father . . .

John T. Ames

Easter

Confession

On this day of days, O Lord, the Easter light of your presence almost blinds us. We confess that we have grown used to the darkness and have even learned how to turn it to our advantage. There are times when we would have preferred Jesus to have remained in the tomb, preferred that he not have appeared to Mary, or to the disciples, or to many faithful witnesses. Forgive us, we pray, our lack of faith, our refusal to accept the mystery and wonder of this day. This day makes every day a gift. Help us to receive this gift that we might serve you gladly all our days, and in the end be gathered with all the faithful ones in your kingdom of glory. This we ask in the name of Jesus Christ, who, though crucified, dead, and buried, lives and reigns with you and the Holy Spirit, ever one God, world without end. Amen.

Thomas W. Currie III

God of glory and might, we admit that though we sing praises to your name when we worship, there are times when our actions do not bring praise to you. We confess the times we treat others with harshness or anger or insensitivity. There are times we judge others or gossip idly, bringing hurt instead of love. Other times we refuse to act in compassion because it would mean going out of our way. Forgive us, God. Help us to praise you not only with our voices but with our living, so that the risen Christ may be glorified. Amen.

Susan R. Tomlinson

On this day of resurrection and hope, we come to you, O God, because only you can make our lives complete. Without you we live lives that obscure your light. We take so much in our lives for granted, and so the least little things can plunge us into worry, fear, sadness, or despair. Too often we fail to live with resurrected hearts—hearts that look around and see possibilities from you, even in the midst of turmoil and turbulence. Just as the disciples were plunged into despair on Good Friday and failed to see the possibility of Easter coming, we fail to see your providence in our darkest times. Help us to form Easter hearts that see possibility and providence in everything, and to form thankful hearts that recognize your hand throughout our lives. In Christ's name we pray. Amen.

N. Graham Standish

Assurance of Pardon

This is a day of celebration, for on this day God revealed the depth of God's grace. For when everything seemed dark and all hope seemed to be sucked out of the world, God revealed the truth that truly nothing can separate us from the love of God: neither powers nor depths, nor darkness, nor death. When we give our lives to Christ, we discover this same promise. God is with us always, shining light in the darkness.

N. Graham Standish

Living God, you rolled the stone away and called Jesus from death to life. We confess that we have set stones before the entrance to ourselves—stones of skepticism that keep us from trust, stones of selfishness that prevent us from sharing, stones of preoccupation that trap us within ourselves. Behind those rock barriers we are dying from isolation, futility, and hopelessness. By your forgiveness, roll away the stone of our sin. Call us from the death of our own making to the life you offer through Christ. Amen.

Mary Marple Thies

On the familiar roads of our daily lives, O God, we have at times stumbled along, deeply discouraged. Sometimes we have been near the edge of despair, wondering if life is even worth living. Then have come those incredible moments when Jesus himself joined us on the road, and our lives were changed forever. Give us minds to know him, hearts to love him, faith to follow him, and the strength to serve him; for it is in his blessed name that we pray. Amen.

Mark H. Landfried

Intercession and Supplication

Holy One, beyond our imagining and imaging and closer than our hands and feet, we acknowledge a measure of dread at Eastertide. Even if we have lost our taste for chocolate bunnies, we shrink from that enthusiasm that a glass of the kingdom's new wine might bring. Even if spring's annual return is not sufficient assurance that death does not have the last word, we fear the implications of new life more than we abhor the deadliness of our rutted passing away of the days. Ignite in us today the burning hearts of those who walk with the risen Christ. Inspire our worship and our daily living with the triumphant faith that, because of Easter, our labors are not in vain. Move us to the laughter that goes beyond cynical sneers and gallows humor because it knows the extravagant joy of the gospel hope; through Jesus Christ our life. Amen.

C. Eric Mount Jr.

O God, who brought again from the dead our Lord Jesus, the great shepherd of the sheep, we pray:

> For those whose crucifixions continue with no Easter in sight—
> Tortured prisoners
> Abused children
> Battered women
> Stricken families of the disappeared
> Homeless poor
> Imperilled refugees
> Victims of discrimination and oppression
> Victims of war

Take your Easter people to the world's crosses to take people down.

> We pray for those who continue the crucifixions with no Easter in sight—
> Because they think people deserve what they dish out
> Because they are just obeying orders
> Because they are just doing their jobs
> Because they are getting rid of troublemakers
> Because they are defending national security
> Because they are protecting sacred values as they define them.

Take your Easter people to the world's hurters to free them from their own bondage.

We pray for those who languish in tombs with no Easter in sight—
  Tombs of their own depression and despair
  Tombs of their own ignorance and misconception
  Tombs of their own narrowness and provincialism
  Tombs of their own isolation and accommodation
  Tombs of their own prejudice and bitterness

Take your Easter people to all the tombs of human deadness to roll the
stones away.

For yours is the kingdom, the power, and the glory. Amen.

C. Eric Mount Jr.

Pentecost

Call to Worship

As you have called us to be your people, O God, so breathe into us your Spirit, that we may witness to your love by the way we live our lives and the concern we show for others; through Jesus Christ our Lord. Amen.

Mark H. Landfried

Adoration

Creator, like the breeze of wind in spring's march
    you blow across the plains;
        all the earth
            grows with each breath.

Gathering the dawn, and collecting the
    body of your kingdom,
        molding the global community that will be.

Your entrance,
    like the warmth of sun poured out
        on the morning mist of predawn,
            fills the shadows of darkness
                and gives new light for illumination.

Like the aroma of the tallest of sycamore trees
    that line the dancing brook,
        you are carried on the breeze.

You clothe our senses,
    carpet our hopes with shades of purple and gold,
        the adornment of the One,
            ushered in as the King, who is Christ.

You sweep in,
    bringing relief to parched soils,
        and loosen the grip of winter in the tundra.

You dissipate the smog,
    encouraging us to breathe you in,
        Your sweet *ruach*, "breath of God."

The gulf hears your roar
    as you destroy sandy foundations,
        forfeiting materialistic ideas,
            quickening us to the center of our soul.

Like the lover's breath,
    you whisper hope,
        promising forgiveness,
          and seal us to you
            with grace from your Spirit.

Some days, the salty tears,
    which created our oceans in your own loneliness,
        fall from your face still,
          leaving us to wonder what
            possibilities are availing.

But like the first cosmic light of dusk,
    you are there to greet us.
        So you visit us in the
          evening of our life
            when we sense our work is complete,
            delivering to us your complete peace.

I believe in your Holy Spirit,
    which gives each of us life

> poured out on all flesh.
>> Who, with the Father
>>> and the Son,
>>>> is worshiped and glorified.

Amen.

G. Todd Williams

Intercession

O God, by your grace make us to be more faithful disciples of your beloved Son and follow more fully in his way, not laying up for ourselves treasures on earth but treasures in heaven; seeking before all else your kingdom and your righteousness; becoming as little children, not fearing, but believing; through Jesus Christ our Lord. Amen.

Mark H. Landfried

How delighted we are, God of the world, to discover in our pilgrimage through the gospel story that the empty tomb was not the final act in your drama. The last curtain did not come down when your Son returned to the glory that was his. What came down was your Spirit—your eternal presence with your people, with your church, with your world.

And when your Spirit descended upon your people, you had the final word, the eternal word: "For I have loved you so much."

Your love amazes us. Unlike human love, it shows no partiality. Your eye watches over people of all languages and lands. Your hand lifts the inhabitants of all countries and colors. Your help extends to the sinners and the saints. Your voice beckons the wicked and the good. Unlike human love, your love does not fail to forgive what is condemned. Your face shines on us when we stray from you. Your ear hears the whispers of our hearts better than do our own.

We would pray that you would make us worthy, Lord. But we do not ask the impossible, and so instead we pray that you would make us wise. Wise that we may see what is possible. Help us to absorb the light that shines in the darkness. Help us to breathe in your Spirit that inspires the weak. Help us in our struggle to be your body on earth as we stand with those who are oppressed. Help us as we bear the name of Jesus Christ, that those who see us shall in some feeble way see our Lord. Let the whole world wonder at our words and deeds. Some may mutter, others grumble, but some shall see and be glad. They shall see and rejoice, for they shall know that you are our God.

We gather as a small part of your church, O God, to pray for each other and to pray for your church. We pray your blessing upon those who are particularly in need today—for those who are sick, including both those who are healing naturally or through medical science, and also those who will be healed by your final call home.

We pray in compassion for those who are distressed, and we join in the joy of those who are blessed—by new marriages, new babies, new jobs, new horizons, new friends.

We pray for your church. Bless your church, which has lived these two thousand years through good times and bad as your reconciling word of peace and grace to your people.

And bless us as we join your whole church in praying: Our Father . . .

John T. Ames

Ordinary Time

Opening Prayer/Call to Worship

As you have called us to come to worship, O God, so breathe into us your Spirit, that we may bear witness to your gentle presence and your powerful love, for we pray in the name and for the sake of Jesus Christ the Beloved. Amen.

Mark H. Landfried

As we open your Word during this time of worship, O God, let it become so deeply embedded within us that it will ever be present as your strengthening grace in our lives, no matter what crisis may come. Through Christ we pray. Amen.

Mark H. Landfried

Holy God, let the glow of your Spirit illumine those places where we hide in the shadows, trying to avoid the life-changing confrontations that worship can bring. Take away our foolish "Do Not Disturb" signs, and meet us in our places of need; through Jesus Christ our Lord. Amen.

Mark H. Landfried

Sacred Friend
    Earth Designer
Divine Guest within
    We come to celebrate
Not with words deeply spoken
    Nor from hours upon hours spent in vigil
But in response to your compassionate love
    In these sacred and holy moments
May the droplets of our love
    Flow into deep moving streams
Washing the shores of life in tenderness
    Giving cause to keep hope alive
Sacred Friend
    Earth Designer
Divine Guest within
    Hear our words of praise and celebration
Through him who is your compassion
    Become flesh.

Raymond Hearn

O God, how many voices we carry within, and how hard it is to silence them!
You know us—you know how fragmented our lives are, how powerful the
many calls. We are here to worship, to praise, to pray, and to acknowledge
you as our one God. Still all other voices, dethrone all other gods, and prepare us to worship you with our whole being. May we hear your voice only,
in and through our worship. In simple trust we pray. Amen

Sarah Enos Brown

Leader: This day, Holy God, teach us how to love ourselves

People: Without selfishness, conceit, or disregard for our neighbors.

Leader: This day, Holy God, teach us what it means to stand up confidently for our faith

People: Without demeaning others in the process.

Leader: This day, Holy God, teach us how to forgive

People: With humility and love.

Leader: This day and every day, Holy God, teach us your way.

Thomas Vandergriff

Leader: O God, we are not so much tempted by fanaticism as we are lured by apathy and prone not to believe in anything enough to suffer for it or be overjoyed about it. We have grown tired of getting all our visions on screens and monitors.

People: Give us, we pray, the purity of heart that can muster the singleness of will to see you.

Leader: We are deafened and divided by the clatter and clamor of many sounds and voices.

People: Give us, we pray, ears to hear even your still, small voice.

Leader: We are dulled by saturation eating and the sameness of fast food.

People: Give us, we pray, the good taste to know the difference between the new wine of your kingdom and the dregs in our old wineskins.

All: Pour out your Spirit on us that we may dream dreams and see visions, that we may hear good news, and that we may taste your goodness; through Jesus Christ our Lord. Amen.

C. Eric Mount Jr.

O God, we are used to pushing buttons and logging on to make contact, but when it comes to true communication, we encounter mystery that does not yield to adroit manipulation. The calm silence in which we can attend to others and hear them out escapes us. The honesty to face ourselves and reveal ourselves threatens us. Fill us now with your Spirit so that we can be still long enough to entertain some presence that we had not necessarily expected and that we can find the words to make our speech something more than noise to fill the void that we feel; through Jesus Christ your Light, your Word, your Vine and ours. Amen.

C. Eric Mount Jr.

Leader: O come, creating, illuminating, uniting, calming, moving Spirit. Descend upon our hearts. You brought light into the darkness in the beginning.

People: We pray you, do it now.

Leader: You have enabled daughters and sons to prophesy, the young to see visions and the old to dream dreams.

People: We pray you, do it now.

Leader: You can turn a cacophony of sound into pregnant silence and into words that do not return empty.

People: We pray you, do it now.

Leader: You can encourage the dispirited, ennoble the mean spirited, and release those held in outer and inner captivity.

People: We pray you, do it now.

Leader: You can take us where we had not believed we could go, where we have feared to go, and where we need to go to be the people we were meant to be.

People: We pray you, do it now.

Leader: In this time of worship, in this time of our lives, and in this time in history, Spirit of the living God, fall afresh on us. Amen.

C. Eric Mount Jr.

Leader: We bring ourselves to you, O God, as we prepare to worship.

People: We desire to begin and end this hour focused on your awesome presence.

Leader: We desire to hear your voice within us.

People: We desire to grow in gratitude and devotion to you.

Leader: Hear us as we each silently lift our praise and thanks before you [*silent praise*]. Amen.

Susan R. Tomlinson

Leader 1:   I invite you to bow in humble silence as we prepare our hearts before God.

Silence

Leader 1:   Lord, we give ourselves to you in worship. We give you our concerns.

Leader 2:   Name your concerns silently to God.

Silent Prayer

Leader 1: We gratefully share our joys with you.

Leader 2: Tell God the things that bring joy to your life, and thank God for those things.

Silent Prayer

Leader 1: God, there are still unhealed wounds in our lives that sometimes cause us pain.

Leader 2: Tell God what hurts in your heart.

Silent Prayer

Leader 1: We come to you with fears.

Leader 2: Share with God the things that frighten you the most.

Silent Prayer

Leader 1: We come to you in trust.

Leader 2: Thank God for the ways that you have seen God's faithfulness.

Silent Prayer

Leader 1: We come to you in doubt.

Leader 2: Share your doubts with God.

Silent Prayer

Leader 1: We bring you our laughter.

Leader 2: Share with God the times you laughed this week.

Silent Prayer

Leader 1: We bring you our tears.

Leader 2: Talk to God about any sorrows you may be carrying.

Silent Prayer

Leader 1: We feel the love of your presence, God. We feel your gentle touch.

Leader 2: We feel your peace.

Leader 1: We feel your serenity.

Leader 2: We feel your strength flowing through us.

Leader 1: We are nourished by you, loving God. We entrust ourselves fully to you as we worship.

Leader 2: Knowing that you care for us, we offer you the praises of our hearts through song.

A hymn of praise is sung

Susan R. Tomlinson

Touch us by the power of your presence, O God, that, as we worship, we may know what is your will for us, and in surrender to that will may know the beauty of your shalom, with the scattered pieces of our lives coming together in a wholeness where life will be rich and full and free; through Jesus Christ our Lord. Amen.

Mark H. Landfried

The ancient word
    To which we still listen for its wisdom and joyous hope
Is God's promise to make all things new
    Thus can we make a joyful noise
The heavens resounding with our songs of praise
    All who hear repeating the theme
And may God's feet move to the rhythm of our music
    What hope this message brings
What redeeming and reconciling reality encountered
    For God's love comes to us in its mystery
Ever curving back upon itself in hope
    Coming on again and again
With the assurance to make all things new
    Let us now worship this God who makes all things new.

Raymond Hearn

In the name of the Creator God
    Whose breath sculpts the drifting sand
Sways the tall prairie grass
    Molds granite mountain peaks
And breathes integrity into all living things
    Both great and small
I would say to you
    You who have come stumbling over pebbles
You who have come from the comfortable and well worn
    You who have come mind weary and body bent

You who have come from deeds of compassion well directed
    You who have come seeking life reclaimed by God's grace
You who have come sensitive to the fragile nature of life
    You who have come with longings for peace
You who have come recognizing the diversity of humankind
    You who have come to be the people of God
I would say to you
    Know that you are in the presence of God
And whatever you have brought into this moment
    There is cause to offer praise and celebration
To the God who sustains us on our journey
    Let us worship God in humility and with great joy.

Raymond Hearn

People of God
    In this moment
This sacred and holy moment
    May God smile upon our intent
Holding us gently
    As we speak boldly of God's justice and righteousness
As we speak softly of and in humility of God's sustaining promises
    As we speak of the melody that gives life meaning and purpose
People of God
    In this moment
This sacred and holy moment
    As a community gathered to worship
Nurtured by love surrounding
    Which forgives trespasses
And allows for the enrichment of diversity
    Let us celebrate the gift of God's redemptive love
Through him who is our friend and brother
    Lord and Savior, God with us
Jesus the Christ.

Raymond Hearn

Leader: Let us bring the tears of our pain,

People: The smiles of our joy,

Leader: The songs of our hearts,

People: The fears of our minds,

Leader: The hopes for our future,

People: The regrets of our past,

Leader: And lay them before God in praise and thanksgiving and with the full assurance that "for everything there is a season, and a time for every matter under heaven."

Thomas Vandergriff

Leader: In this hour, may we remember others,

People: May we get lost in God's love,

Leader: May we set aside petty differences,

People: And lift up what is honorable.

Leader: In this hour, may we pursue God's way:

People: Do justice, love kindness, and walk humbly with our God.

Leader: In this hour, may we practice love, that it may become who we are at every other hour of the week.

Thomas Vandergriff

Leader: Today is a day of joy.

People: May our eyes be clear to see it.

Leader: Today is a day of meaning.

People: May our minds be open to receive it.

Leader: Today is a day of growth.

People: May our courage be up to the challenge.

Leader: Let us worship God, who supplies our every need.

Thomas Vandergriff

Leader: Praise God, whom alone we worship and serve and to whom alone we give our lives.

People: Praise the Lord, to whom "every knee shall bow and every tongue confess."

Leader: Praise God, to whom we belong, in life and in death.

People: For nothing can "separate us from the love of God in Christ Jesus our Lord."

Leader: In praise and thanksgiving, let us worship God.

Thomas Vandergriff

Leader: Let us hold fast to what is good,

People: Rejoice in hope,

Leader: Persevere in prayer,

People: Give joyfully in love,

Leader: Stand firm in one spirit,

People: Strive side by side with one mind,

Leader: And worship God with all our heart, soul, mind, and strength.

Thomas Vandergriff

Leader: Our God is a dwelling place in times of trouble and in times of great joy.

People: THE LORD IS GOOD! God strengthens us with love, so we can rejoice and be glad.

Leader: Often we miss the joy God has for us because our thoughts are turned inward. Let us turn to God with shouts of joy!

People: THE LORD IS GOOD! May God's favor continue to shine upon us!

Leader: Let us worship the God of grace and wonder in whom we are made whole.

Robert Nagy

Leader: In this hour, may we come to worship God with honesty,

People: Speaking truth to ourselves, and to each other,

Leader: Looking deep inside ourselves to discover what is destructive within,

People: That the God of our salvation may restore us and make us whole.

Leader: In this hour, may we come to worship God with honesty.

Thomas Vandergriff

Leader 1:   Eternal God, in this quiet hour of worship we come to bring our tribute.

People: We come feeling rested and feeling tired.

Leader 1:   You say to us, "Come unto me."

People: We come joyfully, we come in sorrow.

Leader 2:   You say to us, "Come unto me."

People: We come rejoicing in our successes and feeling ashamed of our failures.

Leader 1:   You say to us, "Come unto me."

People: We come in hope and in despair, feeling secure and feeling lost.

Leader 2:   You say to us, "Come unto me."

Leader 1:   Eternal God, in this hour of quiet worship we come to bring you our tribute.

Leader 2:   We now silently give you our tribute of praise and thanksgiving, knowing that however we come, we are accepted and loved. [*silent praise and thanks*].

Leader 1:   Amen.

Susan R. Tomlinson

Leader: Christ has opened the gate this morning for us to enter into his life. He stands, ready for us to grow in his way, truth, and light.

Congregation: So let us walk forward in faith, ready to be filled with God's grace and love, and to share God's blessings with each other.

N. Graham Standish

Leader: In the midst of life's confusion, God calls out to us, saying, "Trust in me, and I will make straight your paths. Follow my light, and I will bring hope to your life."

Congregation: So let us worship today in faith and commitment, ready to listen for Christ and to follow where he leads.

N. Graham Standish

Leader: God has called us not only to love one another but also to support one another, holding each other up when we falter, stumble, or fall.

Congregation: So let us be of one spirit this morning as we worship, so that in God's Spirit we can bear each other in God's love.

N. Graham Standish

Sisters and brothers
   People of God
The message to be heard this day
   In great cathedrals, small rural churches, urban churches
In which a people—a rainbow of color, gender, lifestyle, ethnic origin—
   Have gathered to worship
Is God's promise to make all things new
   What hope this message brings
For around every one of life's corners lies something new
   In each passing moment there is something new
For miracles have happened, do happen, yet will happen again
   And within this promise
This trustworthy and true promise
   All the prodigal sons of the world
And all the Samaritan women at the wells of the world
   The people of God everywhere in unity and diversity
Can join hands and become the embodied word of God
   Keeping alive the promise of God's hope
Such is the good news that meets us this day
   Let us then join hands and hearts as a community in worship.

Raymond Hearn

Adoration and Praise

Weaver of truth
    Fashioner of grace
Friend of the lost and the forsaken
    Holy God
We come into your presence
    To give praise and adoration
Celebrating your redeeming and recreating love
    We come hopefully
We come expectantly
    With pilgrims and sojourners of all ages
To meet again
    Your message, O God, of unremitting grace
Through him who is the Christ.

Raymond Hearn

Endearing God
    We offer praise and thanksgiving
When your grace brings softness
    To the harshness of the world
When gentleness is now seen
    Only as a virtue of the weak
When Jesus is resurrected from the safe places of our lives
    In which we have buried him
When all creatures large and small
    Are recognized as containing your spirit
And for your grace, love, and mercy
    That walked our earthly abode
In the person of Jesus, the Christ
    We say, "Amen."

Raymond Hearn

Great Maker of the waves
    That move in rhythm
Determiner of life's currents
    That wash the shores of our lives
Presence of calm
    That stills the restlessness in our lives
We come into your presence

In praise and adoration
For your grace
   That touches the shores of our lives
Nurturing and sustaining us
   For the journey ahead
And when the journey is fraught with danger
   When dreams of the future are shrouded in mist
Your spirit meets us anew
   With a message to keep hope alive
Thus do we pray in thanksgiving
   Through him who is your hope with us.

Raymond Hearn

Holy God
   In the tones of sacred music
In the dance of seasons' change
   Is not each moment a moment of advent
Creator God
   Is not each sandcastle a great cathedral
Parent God
   Is not each breath of life that of a new reality
Loving God
   Is not each word spoken in kindness
      Each hand extended in tenderness
         A testimony to your grace
God of peace
   Is not each weapon we lay down
      Each expression of love without desire for return
A new moment of advent? Amen and Amen.

Raymond Hearn

Leader: We praise you, Redeemer God, for you sent Jesus Christ into the world to save sinners.

People: All praise be to you, Redeemer God!

Leader: We come to this sacred hour of worship in the name of Christ, who died for us.

People: All praise be to you, Redeemer God!

Leader 1: We feel the love of your presence, God. We feel your gentle touch.

Leader 2: We feel your peace.

Leader 1: We feel your serenity.

Leader 2: We feel your strength flowing through us.

Leader 1: We are nourished by you, loving God. We entrust ourselves fully to you as we worship.

Leader 2: Knowing that you care for us, we offer you the praises of our hearts through song.

A hymn of praise is sung
Amen.

Susan R. Tomlinson

Leader: Praise the Lord with awe and joy, for God's presence is with us deeply this morning.

Congregation: For it is through awe and joy that we create hearts ready for God, and lives ready for service.

N. Graham Standish

Leader: Worship the Creator!

People: God creates the skies—

Clouds, sun, moon, and stars.

We worship our Creator.

Leader: Praise the Creator!

People: God creates the earth—

Forest, fields, mountains, and deserts.

We praise our Creator.

Leader: Bless the Creator!

People: God makes the waters—

Oceans, lakes, rivers, and streams.

We bless our Creator.

Annie Jacobs McClure

O God, we praise you for resources of strength beyond all that we have any right to expect. Help us to show our thankful praise as we tell others our stories of your love and grace; through Jesus Christ our Lord. Amen.

Mark H. Landfried

Leader: Awesome God, we sing for joy to you, for you are our strength.

People: We come in joy to worship you God, for you are our ever-present strength.

Leader: When everything in our lives is going smoothly,

People: You are our strength.

Leader: When calamity strikes and life is hard,

People: You are our strength.

Leader: When we are happy and when sadness overwhelms us,

People: You are our strength.

Leader: When we are young and when we are old, when we are enjoying good health and when our health fails us,

People: You are our strength.

Leader: When we are surrounded by people and when we are alone,

People: You are our strength.

Leader: We come in joy to worship you, God, for you are our ever-present strength.

People: All praise be unto you, our strong and loving God. Amen.

Susan R. Tomlinson

Within its translucent beauty
   Surrounding us in its mystery
Curving back upon itself with promise
   Empowering us in its faithfulness
Assuring us that around each of life's corners
   Lies something new
Is the presence of God's love
   Thus can life's sojourn
Be walked without weariness

Lived without fearfulness
And celebrated in joyousness
   God's love.
              Raymond Hearn

Wondrous God
   Of rainbows and empty crosses
Of starbursts birthing new life
   Billions of light-years away
Of humans mirroring
   A serendipity of color, tone, and texture
We come into your presence
   Saying "Amen" for your creative spirit
Making all things new
   We come humbled by what is seen
In awe of the unseen
   As we receive anew
Your promise
   Your trustworthy and true promise
Of grace, love, and mercy
   Praying this through him
Who is our friend and our brother
   Lord and Savior
Jesus the Christ. Amen.
              Raymond Hearn

Endearing God
   In the currents of our lives
That wash the shores of other lives

Wondrous God
   In each threshold we cross
Through which a past is left and a future entered

Saving God
   In the power of love
Which enables us to walk in another's shoes without judging

Surprising God
   For miracles found in simple places
And rainbows not just for our eyes

Compassionate God
  As we exorcise the demonic forces of prejudice
Accepting all others as our sisters and brothers

Forgiving God
  When your grace
Enables us to overcome our phobias

Creating God
  As your Spirit breathes into our lives
That we may hold life less tightly and enjoy the passing moment

We pause to say "Amen" for your grace
  Through him who is your pathway of justice and righteousness
Christ Jesus. Amen.

Raymond Hearn

Call to Confession

Like a nursing mother who cannot forget her child, like a father who welcomes the prodigal son home, so God cannot turn away from us. Though we come, week after week, admitting we have turned from God's ways and have not loved our neighbors as ourselves, God is merciful, slow to anger, and abounding in steadfast love. Therefore, knowing we are beloved children of God, we can admit our failings before God and one another in order to be forgiven, receive new life, and begin again. Let us pray together.

Ann J. Deibert

Confession

God, it is with shame in our hearts that we confess how often we are so wrapped up in ourselves and our own needs that we completely ignore the needs of others and are not even aware of the pain they bear. Forgive us our thoughtless ways. Show us how to understand those near to us, to reach out to them and stand with them in their need; in the name of Jesus Christ, our Lord, in whom we are called to be a compassionate people. Amen.

Mark H. Landfried

God, forgive us for plodding along in our discipleship, calculating with great deliberation every move we make, always concerned for what others will think. Free us by your grace for the surprises of your Spirit, that we may respond out of the abundance of life we have known through your beloved Son, in whose name we pray. Amen.

Mark H. Landfried

We cast ourselves on your mercy, O God, confessing our betrayal of your love, our misguided responses to your love, and our futile attempts at running away from your love. Help us to trust when nothing seems trustworthy, to hope when everything seems hopeless; for it is in the name of Jesus Christ, our blessed Lord and Savior, that we come. Amen.

Mark H. Landfried

When the cutting edge of faith has grown dull, O Lord, remind us of the demands of your love, that we may not only repent of our sins but also bear the fruits of repentance in life-changing experiences that bring honor to your name and the shalom of holiness to your world; through Jesus Christ our Lord. Amen.

Mark H. Landfried

God, we confess that many times we find it easier to talk about you than talk to you. But then as we do begin talking to you in our prayers we often find that talking is easier than listening, and then that listening is easier than doing something about what you are saying to us and calling us to do. Forgive us, we pray, for always trying to avoid the demands of your love. Break through our defenses and use us according to your will; through Jesus Christ, our merciful Lord. Amen.

Mark H. Landfried

You know all about us, O God, even what we think are the secrets of our hearts. Call us from our ridiculous hiding places and open our hearts to your marvelous love, that we may know the blessings of your forgiveness and the benediction of your peace. In the name of our ever present Lord, we pray. Amen.

Mark H. Landfried

God, forgive us for blaming you for every situation in life that doesn't seem fair or that we can't explain. Keep us from self-destructing in our senseless anger, and hold us in your loving care; through Jesus Christ our Lord. Amen.

Mark H. Landfried

Forgive us, O God, for the terrible resentments of life we allow to lodge within our souls, then are willing to have nurtured by every slight we imagine others have done to us. Take away this sinful pride that can destroy our relationships with those around us, even those near and dear to us; through Jesus Christ our Lord. Amen.

Mark H. Landfried

We confess how often it is true of us, O God, that when difficult times come and we are trapped in the little worlds of our own making, we never look up to see the signs of hope you hold for us. Restore to us, we pray, the vision of new life with new beginnings and the promise of your grace in the strength of your love; through Jesus Christ, Lord of life and love. Amen.

Mark H. Landfried

Forgive us, O God, for so easily agreeing that the way of discipleship is the way of self-giving love, while even as we speak the words our sinful pride allows so few genuine steps along that way. Cleanse our hearts by the power of your Spirit, and renew our commitment to show your love in this needy world; through Jesus Christ our Lord. Amen.

Mark H. Landfried

God, forgive us for being so locked into our own experiences in life that we have not even tried to understand the depth of the horrors others around the world have known in theirs. Open our eyes to see something of what they have seen, our ears to hear something of what they have heard, our hearts to feel something of what they have felt. By the miracle of your grace help us understand the ways of your redemptive love in such a world as this, and show us how we can be agents of that love. In Jesus' name we pray. Amen.

Mark H. Landfried

Forgive us, O God
>   For worshiping creeds the apostles didn't write
Forgive us, O God
>   For cherishing traditions whose time is past
Forgive us, O God
>   For honoring saints cast in plastic
Liberate us, O God
>   From laws upon laws upon laws that violate that of divine love
Enable us, O God
>   To recast our traditions in new wineskins
Celebrate saints who are alive
>   Be guided by law as grace and mercy
Find love born anew in the pathway of Christ Jesus.

>   *Raymond Hearn*

O God who travels with us, you know who we are. We long for life that is full and free. We long to know the truth, and we want to leave behind all the things that hold us back. We want to move forward in faith, but the way often seems fraught with problems and dangers. We stand in helpless fear before the complexities of our past and the hiddenness of our future. Stand beside us, gentle Christ. Walk before us, brave Jesus. Call us into life, Holy Spirit. Amen.

>   *Robert W. Abrams*

Merciful God, your law is a gift, but we use it to judge one another as unacceptable. You call us to this time and place to worship you, but our minds wander. You shower us with love, and we long for more things. You create us with talents and skills to share your good news with the world, but we protect what we have in our small corner. You pour out your grace for us, and we pretend we do not need you. Burst through our complacency, transform our narrow perspectives, and forgive how far we have wandered. Set us on the path of discipleship one more time. Amen.

>   *Amy Schacht*

Gracious God, whose love is even more forgiving than it is demanding, pardon us
>   for failing to savor your good gifts while we are experiencing them;
>   for resisting life's transitions as though there were no grace in them;
>   for the acts of unkindness that we have done before we thought twice;
>   for the acts of caring that we have left undone until the opportunity was gone;

for allowing our vision to be foreshortened to now and ours;
for inability both to laugh at politics and to take it seriously;
for reticence about expressing faith, hope, and love;
for readiness to give sway and voice to mistrust, despair, and apathy;
for avoiding the silence faced in solitude;
for avoiding the commitments required in community;
for ever acting as though we are ultimately alone.
We pray not only for pardon because of what we are and are not and because
of what we do and do not; we pray for power—the power of your Spirit—
so that we shall be enabled to be different and so that tomorrow need not be
a repetition of yesterday; through Jesus Christ our Lord. Amen.

C. Eric Mount Jr.

One: Great and gracious God, we find it hard to brave the darkness, much less to see the light in the midst of it.

All: Renew our capacity for care. Embolden us to overcome our fear of the dark because of the light that shines there. Heal our apathy so that we may feel others' pain.

One: We find it hard to wait, much less to hope. Our expectations invite disillusionment more than they create new possibilities.

All: Renew our capacity for hope. Teach us the expectancy that does not weary in waiting. Heal our despair so that we can know a good thing when we see it.

One: We find it hard to stand in awe, much less to bow down. We wonder about problems far more than we marvel at mysteries. In our smug sophistication, we are hard to surprise or impress.

All: Renew our capacity for wonder. Enable us to marvel at the mystery of your coming to us. Heal our blindness so that we may see the light.

One: We find it hard to come to the light, much less to walk in it. We fear being exposed for what we are. In our pretensions, we prefer the cover of deception.

All: Renew our capacity for honesty. Embolden us to overcome our fear of the light because of the forgiveness that comes with its glare. Heal our dishonesty so that we may willingly walk in the light.

One: In the name of the Father, the Son, and the Holy Spirit,

All: Amen.

C. Eric Mount Jr.

Forgive us, Good Lord, for what we waited to do until it was too late, for what we mistakenly did before we thought twice, for what we were able to do because we ceased to see others as persons, for what we were unable to do because we failed to see our own possibilities, for what we pretended we could control when we should have stood in awe, for what we feared, which should have been belittled and overcome. Make us new so that we may begin anew; in the name of Jesus the Christ. Amen.

C. Eric Mount Jr.

Great and gracious God, forgive us for the manifestations of envy in our lives. We have begrudged others their advantages. We have damned others with faint praise. We have sold ourselves short because of our preoccupation with what others have. We have been saddened by others' recognition. We have resented others' promotions and accolades. We have expected others to be content with far too little. We have been small minded when we should have been too big for that. We have failed to be grateful for your amazing grace.

Convince us again that your grace makes riches of our poverty, makes poverty of our riches, and closes the gaps that we accentuate between haves and have-nots. Turn our sorrow into joy. Turn our ingratitude into generosity. Turn our feeling of being left out into faith that we are enfolded. Turn us into the brothers and sisters that we were born to be, are called to be, and can be enabled to be; through Jesus Christ our Lord. Amen.

C. Eric Mount Jr.

Gracious God, whose love is persuasive and not coercive, we confess that we are part of a culture that confuses lust for love, that ignores or even condones the mentality that thinks love is a way of mastery instead of the way of mutuality. Turn us from trying to have our way with each other and with you, from trying to make love instead of being open to love's remaking of us. Teach us to shun domination for dialogue, to eschew manipulation out of respect, and to oppose every form of abuse or exploitation of others.

Forgive us, change us, enable us, we pray, by the love that has sought us in Jesus the Christ, and renew us through the Holy Spirit. Amen.

C. Eric Mount Jr.

Gracious God, you are the very definition of love, and we are the frequent distorters of it.

Love is patient, but we want what we want when we want it.

Love is kind, but kindness can be manipulative, and it can even make us suspicious and uneasy.

Love is not envious or boastful or arrogant or rude, but we would like to be number one.

Love does not insist on its own way, but if we do not look out for ourselves, who will?

Love is not irritable or resentful, but what if we are having a bad day?

Love does not rejoice in wrongdoing but rejoices in the truth, but we get put out and keep score.

Love bears, believes, hopes, and endures all things, but no one is going to take advantage of *us*.

Love never ends, but at some point we have to opt out.

We offer our excuses for love to experience the forgiveness, the refining fire, and the inspiration of your love, O God, that we may die more to sin and live more and more to righteousness, through Jesus Christ our Lord. Amen.

C. Eric Mount Jr.

Forgive us, O Lord, for our nerve and our failures of nerve, for the presumption that sails only on our own wind and for the despair that abandons ship.

We have allowed privilege to anesthetize us.

We have allowed complexity to paralyze us.

We have allowed labels and slogans to blind us.

We have allowed conformity to imprison us.

We have allowed discouragement to defeat us.

We have allowed people to be reduced to objects.

We have allowed mysteries to be reduced to problems.

We have allowed problems to reduce us to indifference.

Leave us not content in our lack of faith and love and hope, we pray, but by your faithful love reconcile us and renew us, that we may live as those who have been both shaken by judgment and empowered by pardon. In Jesus' name we pray. Amen.

C. Eric Mount Jr.

Good God,

Just when we were congratulating ourselves on not being among the hungry, or thirsty, or naked, we read that Jesus is one of these. If not being with them is not being with you, we may be worse off than we thought. Move us and our political and religious leaders to be with them to help them and to let them help us.

Just when we are enjoying not being strangers or outsiders, we read that Jesus is one of those too. We wonder now if our fear of taking them in lest we be taken in has kept us from receiving you. Awaken us to our own estrangement and move us toward those who need to be received into our community and those whom our communities need to receive.

Just when we feel pleased and relieved that we aren't sick, we read that Jesus is one of these too. We wonder now whether we put the ill and dying out of sight and often out of mind in order to be rid of reminders of our own psychological instability, frailty, and mortality. Maybe we are afraid something would rub off if we were with them. Have we kept ourselves not only from them but also from you, and from the sick and dying person in ourselves by our withdrawal? Help us and our religious, political, and medical leadership to be with them and help them and let them help us.

And then we read that Jesus is one of the prisoners too. Couldn't we keep our distance from people like that and still be with you? Are we supposed to feel guilty because a lot of people have been imprisoned, abused, and tortured for their convictions and we doubt we have the guts to stand up and be counted at that cost? Is it our fault that most American prisoners are poor and black or brown, and that white collar criminals get off lightly? Help us and our policy makers to be with prisoners, and help them and let them help us.

Do all "these" mean we are supposed to identify with the least of all sorts—the least appreciated, least cared for, least noticed, least attractive, least promising, least accepted, as well as the least fed, clothed, and privileged? We were afraid of that. O God, by your power, help us to get with them and become your means of reaching them. Don't let us try to use them as our way to you, but help us truly to serve you so that your will may be done. We pray in the spirit of the One who was rich, yet for our sakes became poor, that we through his poverty might be rich. Amen.

C. Eric Mount Jr.

O God, we confess our guilty sounds and our guilty silences.

We have used noise and feverish activity in order to keep from being still on the chance that we might know you.

The sounds of our feuding and fighting, our going and coming, our building and destroying fill our days without fulfilling them.

We make noises and think we are talking to each other.

We make faces and think that we understand each other.

Yet we find it hard to make a joyful noise to you.

We find it hard to say anything candid for fear that we will expose what we are to others or to ourselves.

We find it hard to say anything compassionate without its being condescending or contrived.

We find it hard to say anything courageous for fear that it will bring suffering or conflict.

If we cannot communicate with each other, how can we hope to speak to you? Pardon us, we pray, and open our lips, that our mouths may proclaim your praise and speak your will; through Jesus Christ our Lord. Amen.

C. Eric Mount Jr.

O God, you prepare a table for us, and we want to assign seats.

You offer a banquet, and we want to write the guest list.

You invite, and we make excuses.

You provide enough, but we want more than enough and watch others lack enough.

We consume but fail to give thanks.

We consume but fail to share the bounty.

We consume but fail to share the load.

We are offered a sacrament, but we manage to turn it into a sacrilege.

We set our own tables that you rightly overturn.

Forgive us our table manners. Turn our meals into celebrations. Turn our feasts into fellowship. Turn our consumption into communion. Turn our table fare into justice. Enable us to be the body of Christ, because we see the body of Christ in others and therefore receive the body of Christ as we commune together, through Jesus Christ our Lord. Amen.

C. Eric Mount Jr.

Leader: Let us ask God to forgive us.

Unison: Gracious God, forgive us

For the indulgence that locates freedom outside of limits;

For the indifference that stops caring to avoid the pain;

For the despair that acts on our fears instead of our hopes;

For the distrust that clutches old securities to avoid the risks in making things new;

For the narrowness that makes blinders of our viewpoints;

For the broadness that equates being tolerant with seeking justice;

For the smallness that constricts the circles of our love;

For the loftiness that loses sight of the view from below.

Turn us around, we pray, and empower us to live more as your people are called to live; through Jesus Christ our Lord. Amen.

C. Eric Mount Jr.

"All we like sheep have gone astray; we have turned everyone to his own way." As was true of Israel, so it is also true of us, O Lord: We perish without your grace. Forgive us our tedious complaining and the murmurs of self-will. Forgive us most of all our lack of joy, our unwillingness to hope, our weariness with what is good and true and kind. Grant us that happiness which comes from following Jesus Christ, that happiness which passes all understanding and rejoices in the good of neighbor. We pray in the name of the one who has already redeemed the world. Amen.

Thomas W. Currie III

Help us to remember, O Lord, for we seem to practice forgetting. We forget who made us and why, we forget your daily grace and unremitting love, we forget your forgiveness of ourselves and our neighbors. We forget so much because there are some things we remember too well: perceived injustices done to us, times of betrayal and cowardice we try to keep hidden, moments of envy and pride of which we are ashamed. Forgive our sins, our sins of forgetting and remembering, and help us, we pray, to trust in him who buries all our sins deep in the tomb of his own death and raises us up daily to a life of happy service in Jesus Christ. In his name we pray. Amen.

Thomas W. Currie III

Holy God, triumphant Christ, hear our prayer. We are a nation of abundance and scarcity. We have an abundance of things but a scarcity of satisfaction. We have an abundance of desires but a scarcity of understanding, an abundance of confidence but a scarcity of compassion. We cry out, obsessively, violently, painfully. Hear our cries.

We are a people of strengths and weaknesses. We are strong in our inquisitiveness but weak in humility. We are strong in our reach but weak in our grasp, strong in our hope but weak in our steadfastness. We suffer in our weakness—physically, mentally, spiritually. Comfort and heal us we pray.

We are individuals with joys and sorrows. We mourn the fragility of life, grieve the sad consequences of our actions, and lament the results of our silence. Help us rejoice in Christ's promise of eternal life, minister this day in faithfulness to Christ's call, and experience true peace through a just and righteous spirit.

God, in Christ's name hear our prayer. Amen.

Curtis A. Kearns Jr.

Creator of love and forgiveness, we do not believe that you see us as miserable sinners, but we know that sometimes we fail you. You have commanded us to love others as we love ourselves, yet sometimes we fail to love ourselves. At other times we allow self-love to become self-centeredness. When that happens, we no longer place you in the center of our lives, and we can no longer be channels of your love, reaching out to your children close at hand and far away. Forgive us for loving you and ourselves too little. Open us to the most powerful love in the universe, that you may fill our lives and guide our decisions and footsteps; in the name of greatest gift of love ever given. Amen.

Sarah Enos Brown

God, you are our loving Parent. We know you have gifted us with life, with bountiful blessings, and with salvation in Christ. We believe that everything we are and have belongs to you. We confess that there are many times we do not live as if we really believe that. We give of ourselves and substance grudgingly, or we simply give you what is left over. We are often not satisfied with what we have. We let our own desires for pleasure overshadow the genuine needs of the hurting people of this world. Help us, generous God, to use your gifts wisely so that your goodness may be shared with all. Amen.

Susan R. Tomlinson

God of great compassion, we praise you, for you have forgiven us in Jesus Christ. We thank you, because you are patient with us when we stumble and love us when we act in unlovable ways. We know that you ask us to do the same. We confess today that forgiving is sometimes very hard. There are some wrongs that have been done to us that truly seem unforgivable. We do not always want to forgive. Often we would rather nurse our anger and hold a grudge than forgive. Help us, God, for we really do desire to be the forgiving people that you have freed us to be; in the name of Christ we pray. Amen.

Susan R. Tomlinson

Glorious God, we praise you for claiming us as your own in Jesus Christ. We understand that along with the blessings of being your children you have given us responsibilities: You ask us to forgive as we have been forgiven, to love as we have been loved, to reach out to strangers and help those in need. We confess the times we ignore these joyful responsibilities, wanting only personal blessings. Please forgive us and help us to depend upon you more and more so that more and more we can reach beyond ourselves with the love of Christ. Amen.

Susan R. Tomlinson

God, we know that you have called us to be your people and that you love us with an everlasting love. We thank you that you guide us through all of life. But God, life can sometimes be very discouraging. We do not always recognize your presence or accept your power. We often wallow in discouragement and doubt, weakening our ability to live as your people in the world. Please forgive us. Help us to trust you more fully, for the sake of Christ. Amen.

Susan R. Tomlinson

Leader: You have loved us, O God, with a sure and steadfast love. We desire to live always as your people, but we know that there are times when we fall short.

People: Forgive us those times, Holy God.

Leader: When we do not nurture our relationship with you through prayer and study of your Word,

People: Forgive us, Holy God.

Leader: When we hold envy, jealousy, bitterness, and unforgiveness in our hearts,

People: Forgive us, Holy God.

Leader: When we work only for our own gain and glory, rather than to bring glory to your name,

People: Forgive us, Holy God.

Leader: When we feel your Spirit urging us to reach out to someone in need and we ignore that urging,

People: Forgive us, Holy God.

Leader: Forgive us, holy and merciful God.

People: And help us to give ourselves more wholly to you.

All: Amen.

Susan R. Tomlinson

Lord God, you have given us a wonderful message—the message of salvation in Christ Jesus—to proclaim to the world. Forgive us when we are too timid to share that message. Forgive us when we are afraid our words might bring scorn, anger, or ridicule from others. Help us to use the boldness and strength you have given us so that others may experience the saving grace of Jesus Christ. In Christ's name, and for the sake of this gospel, we pray. Amen.

Susan R. Tomlinson

Loving God, we confess the times in which the excitement of being in relationship with you is overshadowed by the routines of life. We keep ourselves so busy with activities we consider to be important that our joy of being in your presence is often diminished. We confess that we seldom set aside as much time alone with you as we really need. Forgive us, God. Help us to be as excited about our relationship with Christ as we are by so many of our social activities. Help us to live more fully for and with you through Christ. We pray in Christ's name. Amen.

Susan R. Tomlinson

Lord God, you alone are holy and full of majesty. You deserve our honor and praise. We confess that there are times when we honor and praise you only with our lips. Forgive us when our mouths speak your praise but we do not seek your face daily. Forgive us when our mouths speak your praise but we utter slander or gossip about one of your children. Forgive us when our mouths speak praise but we ignore the injustice in the world. Help us, Holy God, to praise you not only with our voices but with the just actions of our lives, that you may be glorified in all we do. Amen.

Susan R. Tomlinson

Generous God, we praise you, for our lives are filled with blessings. We confess that we have a tendency to dwell on the negatives in our lives instead of counting our blessings. We are often too quick to grumble when things don't go our way and too slow to give you thanks for answered prayer. We are often jealous of the blessings of others. Please forgive us, God. Help us to be a more thankful people so that your glory may shine forth in our lives. Amen.

Susan R. Tomlinson

Great God, we know you are the Creator of all that is. We know you have lovingly created us in your image and called us good. We confess the ways in which we show lack of love for ourselves. We sometimes misuse the bodies you have given us through abuse of alcohol or drugs or overeating. We often don't allow ourselves the amount of sleep we need. We show lack of care for ourselves through overworking. We don't spend time with you, thus cutting off our spiritual source of wellness. Forgive us and help us to value ourselves as your precious children. Amen.

Susan R. Tomlinson

Leader: We confess to you, merciful God, the times that we are lacking in compassion for those who hurt. Our judgmental attitudes toward people who are hungry or homeless,

People: We confess to you, merciful God.

Leader: Our lack of concern for people with disabilities,

People: We confess to you, merciful God.

Leader: Our fear of and prejudice against people suffering from mental illness,

People: We confess to you, merciful God.

Leader: Our lack of sympathy for men, women, and children living in abusive family situations,

People: We confess to you, merciful God.

Leader: Our neglect of people who grieve,

People: We confess to you, merciful God.

Leader: Our need to turn a deaf ear to the victims of war and starvation in other countries,

People: We confess to you, merciful God.

Leader: Forgive us, merciful God. And help us to follow the command of Jesus to help those who hurt. Amen.

Susan R. Tomlinson

Gracious God, you have saved us and called us to be your ministers of love and warmth in this hurting world. Forgive us when we do not minister in your name. Sometimes we say we are way too busy, when we really know that this is just an excuse. Other times we do not believe we are good enough for certain tasks of caring. Sometimes we are scared that we will do or say the wrong things. And sometimes we just don't want to be bothered. Help us to understand your calling in our lives. Help us boldly to reach out to spread your goodness. We pray in the name of Christ, who loved us with his whole self. Amen.

Susan R. Tomlinson

Loving God, you are our shield and our defender. Over and over again you have shown your faithfulness to us. Even so, there are many times we do not trust you completely. When the worries of life lead us to despair, we are not trusting you. When we seek answers everywhere but from you, we are not trusting you. Forgive us, loving God. Help us to trust you more so the world will see your work in us. Amen.

Susan R. Tomlinson

Leader: Mighty God, you offer us your power for living through our risen Savior. There are many ways in which we reject your power in our lives.

People: We confess our sin to you, O God.

Leader: When we make decisions without seeking your will,

People: We reject your power, O God.

Leader: When we refuse to take risks for the sake of spreading your love and your goodness,

People: We reject your power, O God.

Leader: When we hide through the use of too much alcohol, food, or drugs,

People: We reject your power, O God.

Leader: When we do not take the support offered to us by the Christian community,

People: We reject your power, O God.

Leader: When we cling to our own guilt, refusing to forgive ourselves,

People: We reject your power, O God.

Leader: You have assured us of your forgiveness and love in Christ Jesus.

People: Help us to live the free and abundant life that Christ offers us.
Amen.

Susan R. Tomlinson

Generous God, you daily give of your bounty to us. We confess that we do
not show our thankfulness by the way we live. We take your blessings for
granted by not stopping daily to thank you. We too often share of our substance sparingly. We are too seldom willing to share our time and talents.
Help us to live lives of gratitude that will further Christ's work on earth. Amen.

Susan R. Tomlinson

Holy God of truth and light, through Christ you invite us to walk by the narrow path and to enter your sheepfold, your rest. You invite us to live a life
of commitment to you, filled with the fire of faith. But the truth is that too
often we are hesitant, and so are only tepid in our faith. We know that your
way is the best, but it is also confusing and unknown. If we walk your path,
we aren't certain where it will lead or what will happen to us. So we avoid
entering by your gate of commitment. We poke our heads in to look around,
but resist placing our whole selves in your sheepfold. Help us to overcome
our fears and our caution so that we can become people filled with your Spirit
and guided by your presence. In Christ's name we pray. Amen.

N. Graham Standish

Assurance of Pardon

Christ's way is simple, but it is also not easy. To walk the narrow path, we
need to be people of commitment and faith, always seeking God's way. We
have been given an assurance, though. When we decide to walk Christ's path,
even though it is unknown, we find that it is filled with new possibility, hope,
grace, and God's blessings. This is the promise of Christ. Through God, all
things are possible.

N. Graham Standish

Holy Lord, in Christ you gave us the complete model of how to be people
of faith. You showed us that the way of faith is to follow you completely,
even unto darkness, trusting that your grace and power can overcome anything. You showed this to be true in Jesus, who said to you, "Not my will,
but thy will be done," and you responded with the glory of the resurrection.
This same offer of hope and glory is given to us, but we let fear be our god.

We shy away from making a true commitment of sacrificing our lives to you and trusting you in everything. As a result, we only rarely discover the fullness of life that you offer us. Help us to be more committed to you so we can live lives filled with you. In Christ's name we pray. Amen.

N. Graham Standish

Assurance of Pardon

The promise of the gospel is sure and true. Though we may experience times of darkness and struggle, if we turn our lives over to Christ and rejoice in the Lord, God will give us feet like a deer that tread upon the high places. God gives the gift of joy to those who persevere.

N. Graham Standish

Holy God, if there is one area in which we continue to falter, it is in the area of forgiveness. Throughout the Gospels we keep hearing the message over and over: forgive, forgive, forgive. But we struggle so hard to do so. We hold grudges that consume our thoughts and energies. We remember the injuries and wounds others have given us to the point that they can darken every part of our lives. They cause us to feel angry and sad, even during happy and joyful times. We hold onto small little slights and they become like walls, blocking us from really reaching out with love and care, especially to those close to us. We can have such a hard time forgiving others that in the process we shut you out. We fail to recognize that when we let you work through us, it is not just we who forgive but you who forgive through us. Help us to form open hearts to you so that you can form forgiving hearts in us. In Christ's name we pray. Amen.

N. Graham Standish

Gracious God, through Christ you showed us the way of love and compassion. You showed us that we are to be a people united in Christ, of one body, who uphold and support each other. You call us to let go of all division and disunity so that in you we can be made one. But we must confess that we do not follow your ways. We find all sorts of reasons to criticize and complain about others, failing to look upon them with your eyes of love. We find reasons to judge others for the very things we can be guilty of ourselves. We find reasons to turn a blind eye when others need our support, and even turn our backs on others when we need their support. Help us to be people of unity and love who care for each other in your Spirit and who also let others care for us with your love; in Christ's name. Amen.

N. Graham Standish

Assurance of Pardon

God constantly calls us to live in God's kingdom, to be people of love, compassion, kindness, forgiveness, and support. These are things that are hard to do by ourselves, but when we give it over to God and let God show us the way, we will always find that our love deepens while our judgments fade. This is the power that Christ can have in us, for through Christ's forgiving love in our lives, we become more caring toward others.

N. Graham Standish

We have such a hard time fathoming you, O Lord, for you are so vast, so deep, so powerful, and so full of love, yet you are also so subtle, so gentle, so peaceful, and so light. We keep trying to define you, limit you, and create you in our image. We want to turn you into a safe God whom we can control. But the truth is that you cannot be tamed, for you are the great "I Am" who gives to us out of a deep and gracious love. You are the servant God who cannot be enslaved but who serves us in love. Help us to form reverent and awe-filled hearts so that we can truly be people open to your grace. In Christ's name we pray. Amen.

N. Graham Standish

Gracious God, you know more than anyone the depth of the world's pain. You know that in all places there are people who suffer poverty, hunger, homelessness, oppression, and torture. Many complain that you do nothing, but you do. You call on us to be your mouths, hands, and feet, to be people who incarnate your love and make it real for all. It is not you who is impotent, but we who refuse to act. Too often we care only about those we know and those who are like us. We do not care enough for the faceless millions who suffer every day. Soften our hearts this morning and inspire us with your Spirit so that we can discern the ways you call us to care for all people and so that we can respond faithfully to this call; in Christ's name. Amen.

N. Graham Standish

Assurance of Pardon

While we are a people with incomplete love, a people with selective compassion, Christ is always ready to take the fragments of our love and use them to make the world whole. Christ does not call us to be perfect in our love, only willing—willing to grow in love for God and others. The message of the gospel is that when we come to Christ with willing hearts, they are transformed into God's heart.

N. Graham Standish

Gracious God, you continually invite us to become Christ's disciples, learning to live in your ways and discovering how to serve you in our lives. While we want to serve you with confidence and courage, we confess that we often fall short in our discipleship. We want to follow you, but we end up following so many other false prophets. We follow the prophets of "Not now, I'm in a hurry," "I'll serve you when I have the time," and "I'd like to serve you, but I'm worried what might happen." Help us to make you a priority in our lives so that we can share in your ministry and life. In Christ's name we pray. Amen.

N. Graham Standish

Assurance of Pardon

No matter how slow we may be to respond when Christ calls, God is the patient guide, always ready for us when we return and say "Yes." Even if we can only give a feeble "Yes," Christ is ready to take that and build upon it the foundation of a wonderful life. When we say "Yes" to Christ, we will be amazed at what is possible.

N. Graham Standish

We confess, O God, that we listen to voices other than yours. The voice of "easy answers" whispers that we need not accept the cost of discipleship. The voice of "earned merit" tempts us to satisfy our own desire rather than to care for others. The voice of "bitterness" calls us to nurture grudges rather than to offer forgiveness. The voice of "cozy friendship" invites us to love those who love us instead of laboring to build up our community with your gift of unity. Forgive us. Silence all other voices so that we may listen to and follow yours alone, through the grace of Christ. Amen.

Mary Marple Thies

God, you have told us what is most important—to love you and to love our neighbors as ourselves. Still, we confess there are times when we know what is right to do and we neglect to do it. At other times we pretend we haven't heard your word to us and we go ahead with words and actions that do nothing to honor you or care for others. Forgive us. Give us wisdom and strength to turn our lives and priorities around so our lives will give you glory.

Ann J. Deibert

Assurance of Forgiveness

Leader: Hear and believe the good news: God is slow to anger and abounding in steadfast love. God reaches out to us again and again, that we might turn away from what is destructive and turn toward what is life giving. God reaches out to us with forgiveness, assuring us that we are beloved children of God, and equipping us to serve God and our neighbor in the world.

People: God forgives us, encourages us, and frees us to love others. Thanks be to God!

Ann J. Deibert

Leader: The prophet Isaiah reminds us that just as a mother cannot forget her nursing child or show no compassion for the child of her womb, neither can God forget us, God's children. The good news is this: We are loved, accepted, and forgiven; we are welcomed home again and again. Receive this good news and live in peace.

People: We are forgiven! Thanks be to God!

Ann J. Deibert

Leader: Wondrous God, who comes to us in many ways, we turn our troubles over to you, knowing that you can attack a whole sea of troubles with power more awesome than that of a roaring waterfall or a storm-tossed ocean.

People: We also open our hearts to you, that you can fill us with peace like a gentle flowing stream and soothe our fears as the rain cools a sun-baked desert.

Leader: We confess our sins to you, knowing that by your grace and the water of our baptism, we have risen to new life in Christ. Amen.

Bob Haseltine

Intercession and Supplication

Open our eyes to see the beauty of your presence in your world, O God. And let it be not just on those days when the sun is shining but on the days when the storm clouds roll in as well, those days when we have lost our bearings and don't know where to turn or what to expect. Let your miracles of love and grace come through once more as the blessed and startling surprise they always are; through Jesus Christ our Lord. Amen.

Mark H. Landfried

Remind us, O God, how fragile are the ties that bind us to life on this earth and how foolish are the notions that we are in control of all the circumstances of our daily existence. Let us be more understanding of our weakness and more trusting of your strength, more aware of our sin and more dependent on the forgiveness and new life you offer so freely. Let our world be centered not in ourselves but in you, in whom is our hope. Through Jesus Christ our Lord we pray. Amen.

Mark H. Landfried

Make real to us, O God, this world of suffering people: some far away and others as close as our own neighborhoods, even in our own households; some with life experiences like our own, and others with experiences we can scarcely imagine. Lead us by your grace to reach out and touch them in their places of need with your compassionate love, as we have been touched in ours; through Jesus Christ our Lord. Amen.

Mark H. Landfried

God of life and love, with thankful hearts we acknowledge our lives to be a gift of your grace, renewed every morning and nurtured every day in your tender care. Keep us faithful to the challenges this day will bring. Make us a blessing to those our lives will touch, and show us how to receive in gratitude the blessings their lives will bring to ours; through Jesus Christ our Lord. Amen.

Mark H. Landfried

Keep us close to your side today, O God, that we may know the gifts of your grace so freely offered, so often ignored, and so quickly forgotten: the gift of your presence in the lonely hours, the gift of courage when difficult days come, the gift of knowing where to turn for the meeting of every need. We ask this through Jesus Christ our gracious Lord and loving Savior. Amen.

Mark H. Landfried

Calm our troubled hearts, O God, and take away our needless fears, that we may be your faithful presence in this needy world; through Jesus Christ our Lord who is the Way we are to follow, the Truth we are to display, and the Life we are to live. Amen.

Mark H. Landfried

God, be with us as we walk this walk of life, that we shall not walk it alone. Help us respect its limits, meet its challenges, understand its purposes, and know its joys, all in the presence of Jesus Christ our Lord and under his guiding care. Amen.

Mark H. Landfried

Touch our lives, O God, and give us the courage we so much need. Then, strengthened with your powerful love, we ask that you use us to encourage others. In Christ's name we pray. Amen.

Mark H. Landfried

Be our refuge in times of need, O God, our hope and our strength when the world has gone mad and everything is crumbling around us. It is in the name of our compassionate Lord who brings wholeness to life that we pray. Amen.

Mark H. Landfried

As the turmoil in the world weighs heavily upon us, O God, keep us from falling into the pit of despair and dragging others down with us. Help us to see your loving hand still at work in the world, and to respond with lives dedicated to doing your will and showing your love; through Jesus Christ our Lord. Amen.

Mark H. Landfried

By your mercy, O God, may we find words of help for those whose suffering brings anguish to our souls and tears to our eyes, as we see tears of love in yours; through Jesus Christ our Lord. Amen.

Mark H. Landfried

God, we thank you for the beauty and power of your word. But make us keenly aware, we pray, of the judgment it brings when we know its challenge and ignore it, when we hear its call and refuse it. Lead us to the deeper truth that transforms our lives and renews your world; through Jesus Christ our Lord. Amen.

Mark H. Landfried

It is overwhelming to us, O God, to think that we live our days on this earth reflecting your likeness into the world around us. Forgive us, that the reflection is so often blurred and the image so often distorted. Keep us close in our companionship with our Lord Jesus, where the reflection of your love is to be found in all its fullness. In his name we pray. Amen.

Mark H. Landfried

Forgive us, O God, for our foolish pride in wanting to be free from all restraints. Show us how the limits you have established for us are your good gifts to us, that being bound to your holy will can set us free to soar with eagles' wings. Through Jesus Christ our Lord we pray. Amen.

Mark H. Landfried

Keep us alert, O God, for temptations that come in subtle ways then grow within us until we find ourselves in full-blown rebellion against your holy will. Lead us by your grace to the truth that will set us free; through Jesus Christ our Lord. Amen.

Mark H. Landfried

As in your presence we confess the sin and the rebellion of our lives, O God, we pray for your promised gift of new lives—faithful to your purpose, serving your people, and caring for your world. Through Jesus Christ our Lord we pray. Amen.

Mark H. Landfried

As we walk by your side, O God, filled with your Spirit and nourished by your grace, may we know that we are called to be signs of hope in a world that has often lost sight of any hope. Through Jesus Christ our Lord we pray. Amen.

Mark H. Landfried

Come to us today, O God, in the wonder of your love. Live in the secret places of our hearts where we have tried so hard to keep you out, those places where you know us as we really are. Fill us with your Spirit, and by your grace send us out into the mix of whatever this day will bring in order to show your compassionate and strengthening love; through Jesus Christ our Lord. Amen.

Mark H. Landfried

Shepherd of every hope
    Refuge for each wounded heart
Companion to the lost and forsaken
    Amidst the discordant tones of life
And in its moments of great joy
    We come seeking to experience anew the presence of your spirit
A presence we ofttimes take for granted
    Or seek only when life spins out of control
We confess, O Holy One,
    To the times we are so busy with the ordering of life
We fail to pause to hear the secrets of a waterfall
    Or ponder the magnificence of a sand dollar
Or fail to renew our dreams and visions
    Great God, as we encounter our appointed moments of life
Empower us to celebrate its joyous moments
    Finding time to renew our souls
In which to find respite simply to be
    And when in moments of vexation we become mind weary and body
        bent
We pray for healing—of mind, body, and soul
    We pray too for those who suffer injustice
Those who feel they have little to hope in, and
    Comfort for those whose dawn is shrouded by the night's grief
Startle us anew, Great God, with your spirit
    That brings healing from the ashes of our woundedness
May we experience the serendipitous measure of your grace

That calls us to live our lives in faithfulness
Doing your justice, living your kindness, walking humbly in your sight
   And when the path becomes difficult, the journey more than we can
      bear
May your grace upon grace upon grace bring calm to reorder our lives
   We pray this through him who is our friend and brother
Lord and Savior, Jesus the Christ. Amen and Amen.

Raymond Hearn

Redeem us, O God
   From inadequate process
Restore us, O God
   To a full gospel of unconditional love
Forgive us, O God
   For honoring law over gospel
Be patient, O God
   For the unextravagant nature of our love
Enable us, O God
   To see each person as a child of yours
Startle us, O God
   With your unremitting compassion
And as we follow the Christ
   May we experience anew the cadence of the music
Of his light and love.
   So be it. Amen.

Raymond Hearn

Wondrous God
   Of Exodus and Easter
Amidst the discordant tones of life
   We pray you would meet us anew with the melody of your grace
Setting straight the pathways of life
   Those of violence
Of words spoken in hate
   In which love is betrayed
Forgiveness not granted
   Spirit of holiness
From your love may order come from chaos
   Healing from the wounds inflicted by life
Startle us, O God, in each sunrise

    Comfort us in each moonset
Sowing seeds of hope
    For those who have little to hope in, or for
May the gentle ways of love
    Bring order to life
Great God
    As we offer our hands in acts of simple service
And as we take each step in response to a request for help
    Let us not count our reward as our due
Grant us, Holy God,
    Strength never to bend our knees to insolent might
Nor close our minds to the wonder of creation
    Wondrous God
Of Exodus and Easter
    Hold us gently in your love
As we sojourn in what is ofttimes a biting and stinging world
    We pray this through him
Who was filled with your spirit, O God,
    Christ Jesus. Amen.

Raymond Hearn

Creating and compassionate God
    We confess to the times we become so busy with the trivial and the
mundane
We seldom pause to hear the secrets of a waterfall
    Ponder the magnificence of a sand dollar
Sit beneath a majestic oak to renew our dreams
    Listen to the symphony of a bird song
Creating and compassionate God
    In our life sojourn
May we pause simply to be
    Celebrating the "being" surrounding us
Then may we lift our prayers for those who
    Face the anxious moments of life's transitions
Suffer the wounds of gender, race, economic injustice
    Await the uncertainty of a surgical diagnosis
Carry the grief from night into a new dawn
    Find life overbearing as they carry it alone
Creating and compassionate God
    For moments in inward peace
Times of woundedness healed
    For your presence when the journey is difficult

We offer thanksgiving
   Through him who spoke your truth
Lived out the fabric of your grace
   Counted all as his sisters and brothers
Jesus the Christ. Amen.

                   Raymond Hearn

Great God
   Of starburst and simple amoebae
We come from a diversity of pathways
   To pause in gratitude for your abiding love
We come asking that you empower us
   With your grace, love, and mercy
Never to disown the poor
   To include those whom you love in our love
May your wisdom, O God, challenge our complacency
   And may we celebrate with uninhibited joy
Moments when our lover's smile washes over us
   Like a breeze on a sultry summer day
Moments when in our solitude
   A secret is unlocked of life's mystery
And we would pray that we may have peace
   Not of the stagnant pool but of deep, flowing waters
That we would have poise
   Not of the sheltered tree but of the oak deep rooted, storm tested
That our power
   Not be of fisted might but of the seedling reaching toward infinite light
Great God
   Of starburst and simple amoebae
We pray this through him
   Who is our friend and brother
   Lord and Savior, Jesus the Christ. Amen.

                   Raymond Hearn

Surprising God
   The message heard this day
In great cathedrals
   Small rural churches
      Inner-city churches
         House churches

In which a people
   A rainbow of color
      Gender and ethnic background
Have gathered to meet a new dawn with its message
   That eludes our logic
      Mends fractured souls
   Is your trustworthy and true promise, O God,
      That around each of life's corners
         Lies something new
      Within the fabric of life
There are threads of redeeming love
   By which to keep hope alive, called Easter
On this new dawn, Great God, we pray for those
   Unable to see the usual in unusual ways
Who carry deep scars of grief and remorse
   Holding life so tightly that they fail to experience its gentleness
Surprising God, may the message of this day startle us
   With its redeeming and resurrecting promise
By which to keep hope alive
   Our prayers are offered through him
Who is the shepherd of every hope
   Companion to the lost and forsaken
Window of your light and love
   Which will never die
Jesus the Christ. Amen.

Raymond Hearn

Holy
   And sovereign God
Of majestic mountains
   And murky swamps
Of nebulae
   And simple amoebae
Of stardust from which we are born
   And cloudburst in which we are washed
Of this I would pray
   To be released from the conventionalism of the day
In which your creative Spirit
   Has been molded to fit our image
In which your life-giving breath
   Has been recast in the shortness of ours
In which your inclusiveness

Has been confined to the exclusiveness of ours
Holy
   And sovereign God
Your call to be prophetic
   Is silenced by our concern for purity
Of this I pray
   With wounded wings
That I may fly the winds of change
   And in my flight
To hold gently
   Those whose wings
Inhibit their flight
   From the wounds of prejudice
And unwillingness to allow curiosity to
   Fly with uninhibited movements of grace
Of this I pray
   To be granted power to stay the course
Not taking time out
   For sabbaticals
That ignore the issues of the day
   And in my course, O God
Hold me gently
   Yet chiding me to follow your course
Of justice and righteousness
   In humility and strength
Of this I pray
   Holy and sovereign God.

Raymond Hearn

Youth 1: Wars rage, countries are laid waste. Will someone light a candle for peace?

Youth 2: We are called to embrace diversity and to celebrate our differences. Will someone light a candle for unity?

Youth 1: Sometimes life seems overwhelming and despair engulfs us. Will someone light a candle for hope?

Youth 2: We live in a hurting and broken world that needs a touch of comfort. Will someone light a candle for compassion?

Youth 1: Depression, loneliness, guilt, envy, greed, anger, hatred—these represent brokenness in our lives. Will someone light a candle for wholeness?

Youth 2: Money, power, materialism, and success seem to rule the day. Will someone light a candle for simple acts of kindness?

Youth 1: The world needs a model of a better way. Will someone light a candle for the church of Jesus Christ?

Youth 2: In our world where violence creates alienation and separates people, will someone light a candle for the gift of families?

Youth 1: The gap between the haves and the have-nots grows wider each day, and too many of the world's children die of malnutrition. Will someone light a candle for justice?

Youth 2: We judge others by the clothes they wear, the cars they drive, where they live, their age, their color, their beliefs. Will someone light a candle for friendship?

Youth 1: As we pray for peace, unity, hope, compassion, wholeness, acts of kindness, the church, our families, justice, acceptance, forgiveness, friendship, and reconciliation, let us remember that we have been shown how to live these things. Will someone light a candle for the word of God that shows us the way? Amen.

Ann Marie Montgomery

Great and gracious God, on whose goodness we all depend, we gather as gifted people with multiple reasons for gratitude. We come here from comfortable homes. We were healthy enough to come. We arrived safely through others' carefulness as well as our own. If our stomachs growl, it is because we chose to leave home without eating. We can follow the service because someone taught us to read. We came here from desire or habit or both because someone told us the old, old story of Jesus and his love. We are free to assemble here and express our beliefs. We are gathered with people whose fellowship supports us and whose love includes us, and we are grateful for all these gifts. We are grateful too for works of art, for "sights for sore eyes" and "music to our ears," for "the sweet smell of success" and the lasting lessons of failure, for the laughter that tells us how little some things matter to us, for the tears that tell us how much some people matter to us, and for the letter or phone call or e-mail message that tells us how much someone else cared.

How blessed we are, yet how needy we are. We need better eyes for beauty. We need better ears for voices weakened by pain, muffled by abuse, and stifled by powerlessness. We need better noses for injustice. We need to get better at reaching out and touching others. We need to get better at avoiding and discouraging tastelessness and insensitivity. We need the peace that passes understanding. We need to learn to handle both noise and silence with equanimity. We need to be able to live with ourselves and to be hospitable to strangers. We need to be able to face tomorrow and to leave yesterday behind. Help us, God.

We pray for those who can't laugh and for those who can't cry, for those who can't care and for those who are overwhelmed by their anxieties, for those who can't work and for those who can't relax. We pray for those who can't talk because they are afraid no one will listen and for those who can't stop talking because they're afraid no one has heard them, for those who can't give love because of fear and for those who can't accept love because of guilt, for those who are tired of living and afraid of dying and those who are eager to live but are faced with dying. We offer our prayers in the name of Jesus Christ, our Lord, who taught and invited us to pray: Our Father. . .

C. Eric Mount Jr.

Now thank we all our God for the manifold gifts that we have not earned: for the measure of health that we enjoy, for the level of intelligence that we inherited, for the riches of the cultural heritages that lie behind and around us, for the wealth of family love, for the legacies of the church's story, for the resources of our ecosystem and economic life, for the protections of our legal system, for possibilities opened by scientific discovery and medical research, for the support that saw us through, for the tolerance that heard us out, for the encouragement that picked us up, and for the acceptance that gathered us in. How blessed we are!

We offer our prayers today for those who feel overwhelmed by their responsibilities; for those who feel abandoned by those they love; for those whose safety is threatened by war, religious or ethnic hostility, terrorism, neighborhood violence, school violence, or domestic violence; for those whose welfare is threatened by hunger, homelessness, unemployment, or deprivation of any kind; for those whose future is threatened by illness, lack of education, lack of opportunity, loss of loved ones, or despair; for those whose world is a sick room, a prison cell, an abusive home, or a dehumanizing job; for those who feel misunderstood, unappreciated, or trapped; for those whose power holds sway over many lives, those whose powerlessness corrupts as surely as too much power, and those whose neutrality avoids the use of the power that they have and are called to exercise. Take us to the places where people hurt and we can help. Take us from the places where we do not belong if we are to fulfill our calling as your people. Give us, we pray, the love that cares more than it calculates, the faith that trusts that love is stronger than hate, and the hope that will not relinquish its vision of a world full of justice and peace. So help us God, our Creator, Redeemer, and Sustainer. Amen.

C. Eric Mount Jr.

One: O God, whose very nature is love, we give thanks that your love has made ours possible, and we pray that our love may make yours more pervasive. We rejoice that your love knows no boundaries and makes no exceptions.

All: Make us, we pray, more inclusive and accepting in our love.

One: We rejoice that your love is both unfailing and tailored to our needs.

All: Enable us, we pray, to be both constant and imaginative in our love.

One: We rejoice that your love is given to all alike but not to all the same.

All: Teach us, we pray, both to engender security in all around us and to express sensitivity to individual differences in our love.

One: We rejoice that your love is extended without imposing conditions or driving bargains.

All: Inspire us, we pray, to desist from attaching strings and to transcend demanding rights in our love.

One: We recognize that your love makes demands and takes sides.

All: Save us, we pray, from being spineless or sentimental in our love.

One: We recognize that your love does not shield us from the truth that we need to know or shield itself from the vulnerability that caring brings.

All: Dispose us, we pray, both to risk the offense of speaking the truth in love and to avoid the honesty that hurts to no good end.

One: We recognize that your love always seeks justice but goes beyond it.

All: Deliver us, we pray, from settling for less than justice or from doing no more than justice in our love.

One: We rejoice that your love affirms the value of each of us and goes to the lengths of suffering with and for all of us.

All: Empower us, we pray, to love ourselves confidently and to sacrifice for others willingly in our love.

One: We rejoice that your love promotes our growth and refuses to "play God."

All: Embolden us, we pray, to empower and not to imprison with our love.

One: We rejoice that your love forgives without limit and without manipulation.

All: Turn us, we pray, from keeping score either of others' wrongs or our kindnesses.

One: We rejoice that your love has led us to think of you in a parental way.

All: Lead us, we pray, to love our parents and children in a godly way.

One: Through Jesus Christ, who has revealed your love most fully, and the Spirit, who pours it into our hearts,

All: Amen.

C. Eric Mount Jr.

Beloved God, I join many in wanting to be loved. Direct me to the way you have numbered the hairs on my head, and let me count less on human love and more on your love, the only one possibly perfect. Amen.

Donna Schaper

Grant me the art of paying attention, even when I'm bored. Enchant me. Let the magic knock on my door again. When I am overstimulated, understimulate me. Make me make space in my life for enchantment. Amen.

Donna Schaper

I have lived long enough to know long, deep furrows. Some are ruts; others are great rivers. Let me know the difference between good habits and bad habits, and make sure that I know that, through you, even I have the power to change—and so does my church. Amen.

Donna Schaper

Lord God, sometimes we find ourselves in great loneliness. We may be surrounded by people, but still we are lonely. We sometimes think that no one understands us or cares about us. Other times we believe that we are the only ones who have experienced what we experience or feel the way we feel. During those times of deep loneliness help us to remember that we are never truly alone. Remind us that there are people who really do care for us. Remind us that you have promised never to fail or forsake us. Fill us with your abiding presence, that we may lean on you for comfort and strength. Amen.

Susan R. Tomlinson

Gracious and loving God, we give you praise for your abiding care and providence, for this universe—in which this galaxy sports a solar system with our planet in its design—for water and for dry land, for vegetation yielding seed of every kind and fruit of every kind, for separating the light from darkness and granting us days and nights.

We thank you for this night and for the sunset that ushered it, for painters who capture the beauty and the poignancy of a sunset, for scientists who subject its light to spectroscopy and teach us from their findings about elements and sustainable atmospheres, and for those windows in word, music, and architecture that open our souls to sunsets—for all these we give thanks.

We thank you for sunrises too, O God. We grow in this sunrise religion you open for us, ever startled by your light and your miraculous dawn. Like the women who first loved Jesus, we come at daybreak to the tomb, expecting the triumph of death and the victory of the tragic. Because Jesus triumphed over death, your angels keep rolling away doors to the tombs we visit. Your messengers keep telling us Jesus is risen, the day has dawned, that our Savior goes ahead of us, calls us into your future. We thank you, O God, for sunrises.

Now sanctify all our sunrises and sunsets. Forgive us when we ignore them, as all human beings do, even scientists and artists. Forgive us when we mistake the signs for the reality symbolized and worship anything less than you.

Keep us respectful of all your creation—living in its limits, adoring its reflection of your love for the world, discovering its truths, reveling in its mysteries, expressing in cogent terms your gospel of love for each of us in Christ Jesus our Lord. Amen.

Louis B. Weeks

We cannot know you, Great God, but only your benefits. We confess our fallen existence, our proclivity for selfish life and sense of autonomy. We fashion idols and imagine your essence in them. Through your grace given in Jesus Christ and the Holy Spirit, forgive us. Call us to yourself and to joyful life in your creation.

So bind in us the knowledge of your benefits and self-knowledge that we may perfectly love you and worthily magnify your holy name, joining the chorus of your saints through all time and space. Make us literate in Scripture, conscious of our history and culture, responsible in our society, inclusive in our communities of faith, clear in proclaiming your gospel, and centered on the One whom you sent for us and our salvation. Amen.

Louis B. Weeks

O God,
We look and we listen for a word from you
that will give us courage,
that will give us a point of view
which is more than our own,
that will give us strength for the journey,
for however long the journey will be.
Help us to walk faithfully
not minding the far-off scene,
but willing to take one step at a time.
Amen.

Robert D. Young

Thanks be to you, Lord Jesus Christ,
for all you have done for us.
Open up for us the work we should do and
the path we should follow so that
we might rise up and be your disciples.
Grant to us
    the optimism of Easter,
    the patience of Jesus Christ,
    the sense of triumph that goes
with what we believe so that
we might grasp this for our own lives,
for our nation, and for the world.
Amen.

Robert D. Young

We thank you, O God,
that you have not left us alone,
that you are with us always,
that your Spirit that pervades the universe
    resides within us.
Take the dimness from our eyes, that we might
    see and
    see deeply and
    see your providence in our past
    and in our present and
    anticipate your providence in our future.
Show us signs of your presence
    as we talk to others,
    as we meet new situations,
    as we wrestle with problems,
And may the experiences we have each day add to
Our understanding of what it means to be loved by you.
Amen.

                              Robert D. Young

Father,
With steadfastness and patience
Help us
    to serve you and
    to trust you,
    to know
        that the road under us is solid,
        that your companionship
        at our side is for real and
        that we need fear no evil.
Help us to keep our balance
    and to approach each day with expectancy.
Amen.

                              Robert D. Young

Set us free, O God,
    from our many sins and
    failures, that we might
    feel as though a burden has been lifted
    and we're breathing free again

Bless all the ways in which you
    shape our attitudes and lives.
Visit us with goodness and
Give us eyes to see that goodness.
Lead us and help us to follow you.
Amen.
                        Robert D. Young

Dear God,
You are close to us—
    closer than hands or feet,
    closer than our breathing.
You are the God who has promised to
Stay with us in covenants that cannot be broken.
We thank you for Jesus Christ, our Lord,
    and for his institution of the New Covenant.
Stand by us
    in our times of bewilderment,
    in our times of despondency,
    in our times of panic.
Place our feet on solid ground and
Help us to believe that you will lead us each day.
Amen.
                        Robert D. Young

O God,
When we are anxious
    speak to us a word of peace,
When we are bewildered about which way to go
    speak to us a word of direction,
When we wonder about the meaning of life
    grant us wisdom and
    enough light to see one step ahead.
We are dependent upon you;
Open our eyes that we might see
    the glimpses of truth that you have for us.
Where we are wrong correct us,
Where we are right confirm us,
But give us a sense of adventure
    and the joy of the journey.
Amen.
                        Robert D. Young

Thank you, Father, for the hope
that you have given to us in Jesus Christ—
   a hope that endures,
   a presence that you provide to support us.
Give us minds and hearts that can discern
your still, small voice that may be
   in a book we read,
   in a meeting with a friend, or
   in something we hear.
Lead us along the narrow but fulfilling path,
and give to us always some feeling of progress
toward your kingdom because
we commit our lives in faith to you.
Amen.

Robert D. Young

Dear God,
In life or death you are our God.
We measure our lives by years and by decades,
But you are the eternal God—
Without beginning and without end.
Our days are in your hands.
We, your people, are in your hands
And we thank you for this.
Help us to take heart in the promises that
Nothing can separate us from your love
And that there is a peace that belongs
To the people of God.
We give you thanks for the reality of these promises
And for Jesus Christ, who gives them authenticity.
Amen.

Robert D. Young

Dear God,
Be the underpinning to us
   when we do not know the road,
Be at our side
   and help us to rest in the assurance that you
   will never leave us nor forsake us
   even when we walk through

the valley of the shadow of death.
Be our destination
    so that we know the road has an ending
    and the ending is assured
Because you are the end as the beginning.
Amen.

Robert D. Young

We confess, Lord, that you are the Way
and that we need
    the way out of our distress
        and into your rest,
    the way out of our anxiety
        and into your peace,
    the way out of our disillusionment
        and into your integrity.
We ask for strength to be instruments of your
    righteousness so that others
    will know we are Christians
        by our love,
        by the integrity of the words we speak,
        by the order in which we set our priorities.
    When we end up on the road that leads to destruction
        show us the exit sign and where it connects back
        again with your will and your way.
And we ask that you will bless us with your direction.
Amen.

Robert D. Young

We come to you, O God,
As the One who created us,
Who so loved the world that you gave
Your only begotten Son,
Who has given us gifts,
And gives us purpose.
We thank you for Jesus who
    stressed the importance of love,
    died for our sins,
    rose from the dead for our justification,
    forgives us and challenges us.

We thank you that all
Your mystery enfolds our mystery and
Calls us to life and to adventure and meaning.
Give us eyes to appreciate others,
To see gifts in them that will make our lives
So much richer as we seek to serve you.
Amen.

Robert D. Young

Dear God,
Lift our darkness, give us the hope of a new day,
Call us from our wavering,
Call us from the depths,
Call us to higher ground,
Call us to yourself,
Call us to that confident position where you
     are our rock and our salvation,
Call us to follow you
     until the spires appear at the world's rim,
Call us to persistent living,
Call us to courageous living.
Amen.

Robert D. Young

Lord, you have been our dwelling place
     in all generations.
We thank you for your Word
     that lives and abides forever
     and is a light along our pathway.
Give us assurance
     that your way leads to life and
     that you are the companion of the journey.
Meet us at the point of our needs and
Help us to bless others
     because of what you have given to us.
Amen.

Robert D. Young

We wait upon you, O God,
We trust you,
You are the foundation under our feet,
You are the companion along the way,
You take the sting out of our sorrows
    and disappointments and grief,
You are new life when we think
    that all is dead around us and in us,
You are the goal toward which we move—
    that one divine point
    toward which all creation moves,
You have granted a plan for our lives
    which is our joy to find,
    which gives us a sense of worth,
    and a purpose for living.
Amen.

Robert D. Young

O God,
You are our rock and our fortress,
our sure defense against the troubles of the times.
We do not ask to live in a world
where we have no difficulties to face,
but only that the strength we find from you
will be commensurate with our problems.
Help us to feed on your strength,
to find the Bread that is more than bread
and guidance along the way as we determine
which of several roads to take.
May we understand that all things work
together for good to those who love you, and
even though we do not see this
as we look ahead, may we see it as we look back.
Amen.

Robert D. Young

Dear God,
Show us the way
and be at the turning points
of the road and
at every crossroads for us
that we might sense that we are not alone
in the adventure of life
but that you are at our side.
You give stability to the path under our feet,
You shine light on the path so that
We can step out in confidence—
knowing that you
are our eternal destiny.
Amen.

Robert D. Young

O God,
Break through our callousness and our
    preoccupations until we realize
    that we belong to you and
    that you are with us every step of the way.
Help us to handle life
with a certain lightness that comes with faith.
Buoy us up in our most despondent times
    so that we might feel not only that
    underneath are the everlasting arms
    but feel the lift in those arms.
Hold us lest we fall and
Give us confidence about the days ahead.
Amen.

Robert D. Young

Dear God,
We thank you for the created world
In which we live—
For its sights and sounds and colors and
All the wonderful things to engage in
That challenge our minds and elicit creativity.
Shape our attitudes, our thoughts, and
Our actions, that they might be more

Like those of Jesus Christ
And recognizable as such.
Give us purpose that sustains us, and may we play
Our part in the long march of the human race and
Never lose sight of the goal toward which we
Move—
The city of God.
Amen.

Robert D. Young

Dear God,
Help us to magnify your name
    until your presence in our lives
    is bigger than our problems.
Give us the confidence
    that you are with us and
    have promised in covenant to
    never leave or forsake us.
Give us the joy of the journey
    that doing your will shall have
    its own enticements and rewards.
Grant us your peace and a contentment that
    you have the whole world in your hands.
Amen.

Robert D. Young

O God,
Walk with us
that we might always have perspective
about what is truly important in life.
Give us purpose and the assurance
that we are not alone
as we make our decisions
and face difficult times and situations.
Be the sure road beneath our feet and
our companion along the way.
Amen.

Robert D. Young

O God,
We thank you for the power of your light
and that the darkness cannot overcome it.
For all who bear witness to your light
we give you thanks.
Help us
    to speak the truth,
    to show acts of love,
    to have understanding as we relate to others,
    to be kind and gracious in our homes, and
    to be seekers for justice in our society.
Make us more like Jesus Christ our Lord, and
may his light illuminate our own darkness.
Amen.

Robert D. Young

Dear God,
Make us strong in faith,
capable in work, and
good citizens of this great country.
Strengthen our nation—
particularly in these ethically perilous times.
May justice prevail,
integrity be a dominant note, and
leadership based on integrity be the outcome.
Nourish us all to be honest and open
before you and the world.
Amen.

Robert D. Young

Dear God,
Assure us
    that there is a purpose in life,
    that all things work together for good
        for those who love you.
Give us the confidence that we
    do not walk alone
    or make our decisions unaided.
Help us to
    treat life as a gift,

understand the process as an adventure, and
live in faith that acceptance
    through Christ is assured.
Amen.

Robert D. Young

O God,
We come to you,
For you are the God who knows us,
Who has promised to show us the way and
Who has nudged us that we might walk in it.
You are the companion of our journey
And the goal toward which we move.
You are the God who has created all things
And in whom all things consist and have their being.
Make us mindful of your presence with us
Today and always.
Amen.

Robert D. Young

We worship and adore you, O God,
for you have done for us
what we could not do for ourselves.
Remind us of our great debt to you.
From our wandering, call us back
to those things that are eternally true.
Keep us diligent in well-doing and
grant us power to speak the truth,
to love one another, to work for justice,
to conserve that which needs conserving, and
to recognize the difference between good and evil.
Give us the conviction that the world is in your care,
And empower us to work for peace and justice.
Carry us through the days to come and
give us much cause for rejoicing.
Amen.

Robert D. Young

Dear God,
Help us to live
  with faith and
  with optimism and
  with buoyancy,
And to trust that you will be in tomorrow
  as you are in today.
Give us stability when we falter,
Turn our tears into laughter,
Grant us resilience and the beneficence
  of your grace.
Lift us up when we fall and
May the resurrection be a reality to each of us—
Resurrection from
  our discouragement,
  defeats and
  from death itself.
Amen.

Robert D. Young

Father, we thank you for your love for us
Which is undeserved and yet is so persistent.
Give us a keen sense
Of what is right and what is wrong.
Guide us along the path that has sure
foundations.
We thank you for every experience we have
  that builds us up,
  that leads us in the direction of helping others,
  that develops our own abilities.
As we make our decisions about how best to live, and
make choices, and give our time
to worthwhile endeavors,
Be for us the unseen wisdom and the driving force.
Amen.

Robert D. Young

Dear God,
Open our eyes that we might see
that you are not far from any one of us.

You are our God, our Savior, our guide,
  our friend, our sure defense,
  our leader in troubles of life,
  our consoler in times of grief,
  our inspiration when we call for courage.
O God of many names, of infinite attributes,
be present to your people in time of need.
Be thou our vision.
Amen.

Robert D. Young

O God,
You have brought light and immortality
to life through the gospel.
Touch our lives with your light
that we might see opportunities around us:
  ways to serve you,
  ways to develop the gifts you have given us,
  ways to share those gifts with others.
Help us to be mindful of those in need,
Make us patient in well-doing and
optimistic that what we do is
never in vain when it is done in your name.
Amen.

Robert D. Young

Dear God, forgive us when we go wrong,
Deal with us patiently as would a loving parent,
Show us the way and assure us that you are the
companion and destination of our journey,
You provide the spirit with which to undertake the task.
Give us faith enough to take the next step trustfully
and with the conviction that the providence
which we have detected in our past
will lead us at turns in the road.
Bless our common journey and
give us always the hope
that where we do not see the way clearly
you will be there for us.
Lead us day by day in the way everlasting

that we might continue our journey with joy.
Amen.

Robert D. Young

You are the Lord, the giver of mercy,
You are my God, the giver of life.
Breath from your mouth refreshes the weary.
Thoughts from your mind intrude on my way.

I am not alone.
I am not spinning like a top.
I am not hopelessly caught.
I am creatively embraced and waiting:

For ideas to flow,
For power to continue,
For knowledge at the next step,
For words to express my beliefs,
For the right words to reach others.

I accept your will, O God, whether my personal passion is useful to others
or only to me. I thank you for any passion, early or late in time, that draws
me but doesn't destroy me.
    Make this a good, carefree day, O Lord, my Lord, Savior, my Life.
I rest my anxieties in you. Amen.

Robert D. Young

God of all times and all seasons, great and wonderful are all your works.
You set the sun in the heavens to warm our days. You rolled moon and stars
in your hands and flung them across the skies to light up the night. We spend
our days immersed in your love, breathing in your grace with each breath.
As we lay in the little death of sleep, our nights are filled with the assurance
of your presence. Your love is everlasting, and we come into your presence
with thanksgiving and singing, praise, and wonder. You are God for all the
seasons of our lives. As people who know brokenness and sorrow, we are
grateful for your presence. We trust your promises and come in response to
your grace, lifting the joys and concerns of our hearts to you. We remember those who are wounded by life—the ill, the dying, the grieving, those
without jobs, without food, without homes. Touch, renew, comfort, and heal
them, and use us as agents of your transforming love for them. We remem-

ber Christ's body, the church. May we proclaim the gospel so clearly by our words and our life that the world may know your love. We remember with thanks those who have ministered to us and carried the gospel to us, parents and grandparents, teachers and ministers. Finally, we lay ourselves before you. By your Spirit search out and find the places where we hurt, and shine on them your healing light. Uncover the places where we run from you, and gather us home. Mold us, shape us, make us one with each other and one with Christ. Dear God, you astonish us by granting requests that are only half-formed, by enriching our experience in unexpected ways, by reminding us of factors we have overlooked. However our prayers are answered, may the outcome be that we love you more and trust you with greater confidence. We ask this in Jesus' name. Amen.

Mary Marple Thies

God, you hear what I am saying;
you see what I dream.
My only hope is for you to keep listening;
you're the only one whom I can trust.
At dawn I begin to search my soul for words of warmth;
when I rise I want to praise you.
You are pained by my mistakes,
for nothing unloving can reside in you.
Ignorance cannot measure up to you.
Those who oppress others shall
bear your displeasure.
My role shall be that of a worshiper
celebrating your love;
in gratitude I will turn my face to the
cross and altar.
God, lead me in your steps of goodness;
may the road lead me in straight paths.
Embark, all who bear witness to the love of God, celebrate with me.
Hosanna! Hosanna!
You embrace us all;
may we all find complete happiness
in you.
To all those who embrace love,
you give happiness.
Your love is stronger than
tempered steel.

G. Todd Williams

God, you gather us up and call us your people, claiming us as your children, and send us into the world to share the good news of what it's like to be in your family. We thank you for the good parts of being family together: for the strength and support of others, and for the blessings you give us through the lives of our sisters and brothers. In the times when we are wounded by those who are in our family, we pray for wisdom and strength to know how to respond: how to rise up and demand justice, how to speak and how to have patience, how to resist evil and not to rest until no one lives with injustice, and when and how to forgive.

God, you know the desires of our hearts, the people for whom we are concerned, the anxieties we harbor, and our need for healing where there is sickness in body, mind, or spirit. We ask that the healing wings of your Spirit enfold all who are in need. Where peace and justice are in short supply we ask for a full measure. Use us, that our loves might reveal your glory—that through our decisions and interactions, large and small, the world might be transformed into the creation you intend.

You came into this world to be like us, to show us how to be more like you. We give you ourselves—all that we are and all that we have. Amen.

Ann J. Deibert

We are grateful for so much:
For glimpses of peace in our world,
For reconciliation when we have been estranged,
For health following sickness,
For rest after hard work,
For work when we have been unemployed,
For good friends,
For family who are friends and for friends who are family,
For the good news that hope is stronger than despair, that love is stronger than hate, that life is stronger than death.
We thank you.

We pray for those for whom we are concerned. We pray not just for those whom we know and love but also for those who are strangers to us—even enemies. We pray for their well-being. We pray for courage where there is fear, knowledge where there is ignorance, wholeness where there is brokenness.

You call us to be your people, to give ourselves on behalf of others, to expand our resources on substance that matters, such as freedom, justice, peace, healing, love. God, you may even be calling us now to take action— you may have called us to this place and this time because people's lives are at stake and if we do not follow you, many may perish. Give us discernment to know it is you calling us. Give us wisdom to know how to subvert the system of domination that keeps people in their place. Give us courage to speak truth to power. Whether large or small, may our lives make a difference for you and for our sisters and brothers—even for all of the creation that you made in love. Amen.

Ann J. Deibert

Count us among your covenant people, Holy God. As you established your promises with Abraham and Sarah and the generations that followed them, we want you to be our God and we want to be your people. We reach out for your blessing, that we might in turn bless others, that our lives might bear the fruit of your love and peace, that our world might be transformed into a place where you are glorified and where all your creation is at peace.

Until that day comes, we pray for its arrival. Use us for your purposes. Challenge us where we have become complacent. Open our hands where we have grown afraid of giving. Warm our hearts where we have become cynical and cold.

We remember so many—ourselves included—who are in need. We pray for strength in body, mind, and spirit. We pray for the well-being of those whose concerns we know. We pray too for those who are only a nameless face or faceless name to us. We remember the brothers and sisters we have all across this nation.

We give you thanks for anniversaries, for goals achieved, for work well done and rest long deserved. For all your blessings, known and unknown, remembered and forgotten, we give you thanks. Amen.

Ann J. Deibert

Lord God, we come before you this morning with motives mixed, or perhaps with no known motive at all. Yet here in this place—whose very walls are filled with memories—we sense your presence with us. We thank you that it is not necessary for us to wait for your presence until we deserve it, or until we have banished all other thoughts and considerations from our minds. Often when we least expect it, we become aware of you, and when we feel least in need of your Spirit, we find that it is with us.

We thank you, loving God, for the faith that has been awakened in us. We thank you for the conviction that there is, at the heart of the universe, a purpose, a unity, a reason, a destiny, and that this purpose is guaranteed to us by the life, death, and resurrection of Jesus Christ our Lord.

We thank you for the love that you have shown the world through him, and for the love that we are enabled to show each other. And we thank you for the hope that is in us—hope of a better world that you have promised and that you have called us to work for.

Give us your grace as we join together to work for the kingdom that you promise on earth. Let us never rest at peace until hunger, oppression, discrimination, pollution, and war have been banished from our planet. Bless the efforts of those who are working to eradicate these ancient scourges. Unite all persons of goodwill, who perceive your grace in many various ways, as we work together for your world.

We pray that your kingdom will come on earth, and we pray that we may be given the grace to participate at least a little bit in its coming.

We pray that your will might be done here—where demonic powers are still so evidently at work. We know your will—at least we know vast amounts of it. Give us the grace to do it. Help us not to worry about what we do not understand, but to think carefully about what we understand perfectly well: your love and your concern for all peoples, your concern for the natural world that you created and that you entrusted to us, your determination that justice and righteousness shall roll through human society like a rushing mountain stream. May we firmly believe and act out our faith that your will is being done in us and through us.

We pray for daily bread—for life and health, strength and courage—not just for ourselves but for those who lack these basic necessities.

We pray for your church—for this congregation that we love, for the denomination of which we are a proud part, and for all who bear your name regardless of what other name they bear. Especially today we pray for [*names of congregations*].

Finally, we pray for ourselves: for those of us who are sick and who need your gift of healing, especially [*names*]; for those who are in despair and who need your gift of comfort; for those who are nearing the end of their life and who need your gift of faith.

And unite us in the church's family prayer: Our Father . . .

John T. Ames

Eternal God, the world you give us and the life you set us to live are full of beauty, wonder, glory. Please don't let us miss them. No matter what else happens, or however much else must be tended to, please don't let us miss the beauty, the wonder, the glory of life in your world.

Make us discontent with the ordinary things that we so often settle for: cheap entertainment, frozen food, sloppy music, plastic flowers, ugly rooms, sleazy politicians, relationships quickly formed and quickly broken. Teach us the truth that life in your world can be filled with beauty—with the beauty of form and color, of music, of taste, of love.

Teach us the beauty of holiness, give us a sense of awe in your presence, fill us with a passion to be your people. Preserve us from treating you as a celestial waiter or nurse and your church as a leisure time activity or a hobby to be indulged in if time permits.

Make us discontent when we offer less than our whole selves to you. We rush to worship for an hour most weeks, thinking that we have done you a favor for which you should be very grateful. Teach us that all of our life is our offering to you—our skills, our intelligence, our capacity for love and compassion, our whole being. Teach us that every relationship can be divine, that every day's activity can be holy, that all of life can be beautiful.

Fill us with gratitude today for the blessings with which we are surrounded— a world of natural beauty, people whom we love, a community in which we can serve. Make us also grateful for your greatest gift—your presence with us in times of both happiness and sorrow.

Especially we pray for those who gather here in need—those in need of companionship, of reassurance, or of a reason for living. We pray for those in need of prayer, O God, for none of us is able to bear difficult burdens alone. We pray especially for [names] and for others whom we name silently…

Surround your people with your love, as we join in the prayer that unites all Christians: Our Father. . .

John T. Ames

Good and gracious God, many prayers are said, many hymns are sung, many sermons are preached here in your honor and glory. But however much we may try, we cannot begin to say it all. Even what little we do or say only hints at what we feel. Still, it is good for us to try. Our dissatisfaction with our own efforts reminds us of your greatness, your mystery, your splendor. And we know that you have been with us, because we have worshiped you.

But we cannot understand one who is altogether splendor, one before whom we fall down in awe, one whose glory and majesty is revealed only symbolically—through the splendor of your world, through our own better natures, by the witnesses of the past, through the fact that we love.

We cannot understand you, and so you come to us. You understand us. You accept us. You give yourself to us. You love us.

May we embrace life—all of life, the life that Jesus called "more abundant." Open our hearts and minds to all that your love and your goodness have put here for our enjoyment and fulfillment.

Give us a greater sense of love—more capacity to receive from and give to other people, more sense of community, less individual reliance.

Give us a greater sense of beauty—the beauty of your world, the beauty of children playing, the beauty of two lives grown old together.

We pray today for your world and for your people. Especially we pray for those who are in distress today: for those troubled by natural disasters, for churches and other agencies of goodwill and compassion as we try together to help.

We pray for those parts of your world that continue to be ravished by war, caused in most cases by ancient ethnic rivalries and most tragically by religious differences.

We pray for those here who are in need: those in need of companionship, of healing, of reassurance, or of a reason for living. We pray for those who are in need of prayer, for none of us is able to bear hard burdens alone. Be with us all, and especially for those we name silently at this time.

Show us whom we can help. Show us what we can do. And go with us for Jesus' sake, as we pray the prayer that unites us with his disciples in all ages: Our Father . . .

John T. Ames

Special Occasions in Ordinary Time

Baptism

Confession

Gracious Father, by water and the Spirit we have been claimed as children of your covenant, cleansed and made whole in Jesus Christ. Forgive us for preferring darkness to light, for rejecting your gifts and forgetting your love. Forgive us when we have acted as if we knew no covenant and belonged only to ourselves. Grant us the gift of your Holy Spirit, we pray, that we might be united to Christ, serving him all our days and becoming a nursery of faith for each child of the covenant entrusted to us. We pray in Christ's name. Amen.

Thomas W. Currie III

Intercession and Supplication

Holy and gracious God, who pities us like a father and comforts us like a mother, we give thanks for the addition of children to the church's fellowship as well as to our circles of kinship. Made aware of the starvation, suffocation, mutilation, molestation, immolation, rape, deprivation, and discrimination of which the girls of our world are more apt to be victims than the boys, we are thankful that the prospects of [*name*] are far brighter than those of most of her sisters in the global human family. We rejoice that the love of Jesus knew no bounds of exclusion, that he resisted his society's ways of assigning women a lesser place, and that the Holy Spirit is poured out on all flesh, causing both daughters and sons to prophesy. We rejoice that this child's birth into the household of faith affords her full participation in the kinship of your Spirit's bond.

Inspire us now and this little girl later, because of our particular covenant as your people, to make the world safer for the children who are denied daily their birthrights in the inclusive covenant of humanity. Bless, by the power of your Spirit, what we now do with water, that it may signify a spring of new birth beyond the physical birth that has brought [*name*] into our midst. As we are all dependent on your gracious forgiveness and transforming power, wash and renew this child as you do us, that she may learn the ways of love and shun the ways of sin. Enable her to grow and flourish in the faith that has been expressed for her today. Strengthen and guide [*parents' names*] and [*siblings' names*] as they encircle [*name*]'s life with theirs. Strengthen and guide all who will have a part in her nurture and development to the end that your church, our church, her church, may be built up by the love that moves back and forth among us as followers of the living Christ, to whom, with you and the Holy Spirit, be all honor and glory, now and forever. Amen.

C. Eric Mount Jr.

Great and gracious God, we give thanks that you nourish and sustain all things by the gift of water, that your life-giving rain falls on both the just and the unjust, and that we have reason to believe your promise to pour out your Spirit on all flesh because of what has come to us in Jesus Christ and through the Holy Spirit. We acknowledge that baptizing babies seems out of place in the world that is reported in our daily news. Ruled out before birth, destroyed as newborns, ravaged from the start by mothers' malnutrition and drug use, stricken by starvation, debilitated by hunger and disease, tortured by abuse, starved by neglect, gunned down even at school, massacred in war, exploited as labor, robbed of horizons, the potential new citizens of our planet are often terribly at risk. And yet we can be grateful today that little [*name*] has begun his/her life with two loving parents, with two families—his/her own and the church—and with two spirits—his/her own and yours. As we baptize this child with water, we symbolize the faith and offer the prayer that he/she will have two births, not just one, and two names—his/her own Christian name and the name of Christian. As your word, like rain and snow, waters the earth and makes it bring forth and sprout, may this sacrament symbolize the watering of his/her personal development and of all his/her relationships with life abundant that comes from you. Bless [*parents' names*], the other members of his/her family, and this congregation, that all of us may be for him/her a nursery of the Spirit, a school of faith, and a fellowship of love, in the name of the creating, sustaining, empowering triune God in which we live and move and have our being. Amen.

C. Eric Mount Jr.

Gracious God, our former and transformer, our nurturer and liberator, your goodness has splashed down upon us; it has welled up around us and within us; it has cleansed and healed us; it has carried us along; we go with its flow. Our forebears in faith have led us to believe that it was your Spirit that first breathed on the waters and hollowed out a place for life to lodge in this universe. That same Spirit hollowed out a place through the water for the Hebrews' birth passage as they moved from bondage to freedom, from being nobodies to being your body; and that same Spirit descended on Jesus at his baptism to set him apart, and brought his body, the church, into being, hallowing it for its mission. Now in faith we bring [*name*] to you, believing that your Spirit is hollowing and hallowing a place for him/her—a place of creative, responsive, liberating, and reconciling love in his/her family and in his/her larger church family. We do so in the confidence that the same Holy Spirit will enable him/her someday to make a place for himself/herself in your church and in your world. Unaccustomed as we are to talk of holy water here, we still sense that this water is different because of what we dare in faith to do with it. Set it apart, we pray, thereby making it holy. Hallow it as you have hallowed us to be your saints. As [*name*] has been formed in [*mother's name*]'s womb before birth, may he/she be reformed in the womb of his/her mother church and born anew. Pour out your Spirit of the living Christ on him/her and on [parents' names] so that, despite the deadly influences and possibilities that haunt our hopes for our children and grandchildren, he/she may receive and choose live possibilities at each stage of his/her journey toward maturity as a follower of Jesus Christ, the water and the bread of life, in whose name we pray. Amen.

C. Eric Mount Jr.

Celebration of the Lord's Supper

Confession

Our Father, forgive us when we refuse to come to the banquet, when we stand outside and murmur against the extravagance and injustice of your grace. Forgive our silly righteousness, our lethal pride, our efforts to live off the abundance of ourselves. Impoverish us, we pray, so that we might be filled with Christ, with the bread of life and the wine of his Spirit. So may we learn the manners of the kingdom and find our places around the table of your love. We ask this in the name of Jesus Christ. Amen.

Thomas W. Currie III

Prayer before Communion

Holy and gracious God, the heavens tell your glory and the firmament proclaims your handiwork. You are the author of this marvelous universe. You are our maker and not we ourselves. You have made us for yourself so that our hearts are restless until they find rest in you, yet we have not been faithful to the covenant to which you keep calling us. The instruction of Moses, the correction of the prophets, and your Word made flesh in Jesus the Christ have repeated your gracious communication to us. Despite our alienation, waywardness, and estrangement, your steadfast love endures forever. Therefore, we lift our voices in joyful praise with all the faithful of every time and place:

Holy, holy, holy Lord, God of power and might,
Heaven and earth are full of your glory.

Hosanna in the highest.
Blessed is the One who comes in the name of the Lord.
Hosanna in the highest.[2]

We give thanks for the story of Jesus commemorated and communicated in this ritual. We give thanks that, even if no one else knows the trouble we've seen, he did. We are grateful that he shared table fellowship with people others excluded, that he received little children and blessed them, and that he brought health to our affliction, light to our darkness, God's reign to our tyranny and chaos, and life to our death. We give thanks that he drank the cup of obedience to the dregs—even to death—and that he reversed the vicious cycle of retribution, revenge, and violence for us and all humanity. We give thanks that even death could not hold him.

We rejoice that in this meal that he gave us—a meal by which we become sharers in his life as members of his body, a meal at which no one goes away hungry and no one grabs too much, a meal that we have to share slowly together rather than drive through and take out. Remembering your grace toward us, we take this bread and wine from among the gifts of your creation as signs of your saving help to us in Jesus Christ, and we offer ourselves as a sacrifice of praise and thanksgiving to proclaim the dying, rising, coming Christ. Pour out your Spirit upon us and upon your gift of bread and wine, that they may be for us the body and blood of Christ and that we may truly be his body in the world for which he lived and died and still lives. By your Spirit, unite us both with the living Christ and with all your people everywhere, that together we may offer the compassion and forgiveness and healing and hope that have come to us through him. Through Christ, with Christ, in Christ, in the unity of the Holy Spirit, all glory and honor are yours, eternal God, now and forever. Amen.

C. Eric Mount Jr.

Thanksgiving

Everlasting God, we join with your church in all times and places to thank you for creating us in your image and caring for us and all your creatures. When we marred your image through sin, you mercifully did not hold it against us but gave of yourself in Jesus that we might in turn become more like you. Jesus lived among us full of grace and truth. He forgave sinners and healed the sick. He spoke the good news of your coming world of justice and peace.

---

2. *Book of Common Worship*, 127.

He lived for you and gave himself for us—and through him you destroyed the power of sin and death.

With joyful lips we speak and sing to you our praise and gratitude that you welcome us, that you have prepared a place for each of us to sit at your table— elbow to elbow with our sisters and brothers—at home in your family.

As sheaves of wheat turn from green to gold in the summer sun and grapes redden and are transformed into wine, transform us to be a new people bound by love and ripened into the body of Christ. Like the grains that become one loaf, like the notes that are woven into song, like the droplets of water that are blended into the sea, make us one—your body in the world.

> *Ann J. Deibert* (adapted from "Sheaves of Summer,"
> *The Presbyterian Hymnal*)[3]

Generous God, with these hands you give us, we hold these gifts for you. With these arms you give us, we stretch to gather in the lost and alone. With these eyes you give us, we see opportunities to share your good news. With these hearts you give us, we pray for strength and healing for others. You have given us what we need to be your disciples; we give to you all that we are to praise your name. Use these gifts and your people to spread the saving love of Christ. Amen.

> *Amy Schacht*

God, we thank you for times of physical rest that rejuvenate our bodies, and for times of spiritual renewal that refresh our souls. They are a great blessing that comes as the gift of your grace; through Jesus Christ our Lord. Amen.

> *Mark H. Landfried*

We stretch out our hands to you, Lord God, and praise your holy name, confident that you will not turn away from us or let us fall. Receive us by your grace and embrace us in your love; through Jesus Christ, our Lord of love. Amen.

> *Mark H. Landfried*

We are aware, O God, of the marvelous gifts that have come from your hand and have profoundly enriched our lives. But keep us, we pray, from being so focused on the gifts that we forget the Giver. Help us find ways of express-

---

3. *The Presbyterian Hymnal: Hymns, Psalms, and Spiritual Songs* (Louisville, Ky.: Westminster John Knox Press, 1990), 518.

ing our praise, speaking our words of thanks, and sharing the gifts with others. In Christ's name we pray. Amen.

Mark H. Landfried

Though we have experienced your grace in many ways, we are still in awe, O God, at the depth of your compassion and the breadth of your love. Where we give up so easily, as our love falters and fails, your love never fails, for it comes to us through our Lord, who was faithful even to death on the cross so that we might have life abundant and eternal—life full and rich and free. It is in his blessed name that we pray. Amen.

Mark H. Landfried

We thank you, God, for the excitement of the morning when the dawn of a new day breaks and everything is fresh and new. Help us to receive the gift with gratitude and use it wisely and well; through Jesus Christ our Lord. Amen.

Mark H. Landfried

We thank you, God, for bringing us to this day, with all its promise for days yet to come. Lead us into our future with a strong sense of hope, that where you are, we may be also; through Jesus Christ our Lord. Amen.

Mark H. Landfried

We thank you, God, that although the storms of life do come, so also does the rainbow through the rain. Be with us in your compassionate presence and give us trusting hearts; through Jesus Christ our Lord. Amen.

Mark H. Landfried

Majestic God
    As night sounds end
And day sounds begin
    The fluorescent colors
Of darkness and light blending
    May we pause
In quiet time
    To offer thanksgiving.
        Raymond Hearn

Thanksgiving Day

Call to Worship

Leader: Please hear our prayers of thanksgiving, gracious God!

People: We give you our thanks, gracious God, with our whole heart. Before all the world we sing your praise.

Right Side: For wooded hills and flowing streams, for sunset and moon-rise,

Left Side: We give you thanks.

Right: For sunshine, rain, and bountiful crops,

Left: We give you thanks.

Right: For things that run, hop, and fly,

Left: We give you thanks.

Right: For the ability to enjoy your creation,

Left: We give you thanks.

Right: For the laughter of children, the hugs of friends, the smile of a loved one,

Left: We give you thanks.

Right: For productive lives and quiet moments,

Left: We give you thanks.

Right: For the beauty of your presence, the comfort of your touch, the knowledge of your faithfulness and love,

Left: We give you thanks.

Right: For forgiveness through Christ and life everlasting,

Left: We give you thanks.

Leader: For all the ways we see the splendor of your glory and experience your goodness,

People: We give you thanks, gracious God, with our whole heart. Before all the world we sing your praise. Amen.

Susan R. Tomlinson

Prayer for an Interfaith Thanksgiving Community Service

Eternal God, on this day of national thanksgiving, we gather to praise you for the gifts that you have lavished upon us. We drink water that quenches our thirst. We eat food that satisfies our hunger, nourishes our bodies, and gives us enjoyment and occasion to be with people we love.

We feel the sun on our faces, and it is good. We hear the rain on our roofs, and it is also good. We hear the roar of the sea and the geese above, see foxes and turtles, the swan on the pond and ice in the ditches. We hear children playing in the park and see old people holding hands as they walk together. We have dreams in our brains, love in our hearts, laughter on our lips. And they are all very good. We thank you for the world that you created and that you entrusted us to use, enjoy, and care for—as a sign of your eternal providence.

As we gather from many places of worship, we unite in giving you thanks for the community in which we live and to which we commit ourselves in service as your people. We thank you for the people of this community— the old and the young, the rich and the poor, farmers, laborers, businesspeople of many races and languages and styles of life—who worship you in accordance with many different traditions. For all those who contribute to this community, we give you thanks.

We praise you as well for this land of abundance: for the mountains and rivers and lakes, for rich soil and rare minerals, for vibrant cities and the beautiful countryside.

We thank you also, God, for things unseen—not for conquests of the sword but for conquests of the spirit, which have forged out a nation where freedom is enjoyed. We remember those ancestors who dreamed of a nation conceived in liberty and who carved a community out of [*name your particular geographical region*]. We remember our ancestors who met those first European ships, those who were brought in chains from Africa, those who escaped from the ghettos of Europe and the barrios of Latin America. Together they created a land and entrusted it to us. Enable us to live together in harmony, to work together in peace, to strive together to give our children a finer community than we inherited.

And though we are filled with thanksgiving for all these blessings, we are made sorrowful for the ways in which dreams and hopes have been realized. Forgive us for being content when our land is stained by islands of hopelessness. Forgive us for our blindness to needless misery. Forgive us when love of money has calloused our social consciences and our concern for the environment. Forgive us when we assume that everybody ought to be like we are in appearance, culture, and philosophy, and when we consider ourselves superior to those who are simply different.

The things we pray for, good Lord, give us the grace to labor for; in the Lord's name. Amen.

John T. Ames

Marriage and Anniversary

Thank you, God, for the beautiful relationships of life that you give us, for the special persons who make our hearts leap for joy and bring fullness to our days. As we receive love from them and give love to them in a bond that grows deeper and richer with each passing year, keep us, we pray, from ever taking lightly such a gift as that; through Jesus Christ, our Lord, who showed us the breadth and length and height and depth of what love is meant to be. Amen.

Mark H. Landfried

Lead us in our marriage relationships, O God, to reach out with our love to each other in such genuine ways that the potential of each may develop to fullest maturity, where each may rejoice in the other, and where, in the integrity and beauty of such a relationship, your kingdom may come and your will be done; through Jesus Christ our Lord. Amen.

Mark H. Landfried

Gracious God, whose presence brings joy to our celebrations, whose goodness makes our common life uncommonly good, and whose faithful love enables us to give love and keep promises, we claim your presence and desire your partnership in this marriage so that what we seal here will be not simply a legal contract but a sacred covenant. We give thanks for all that has made today possible for [*names*] and all that makes tomorrow promising for them: the love of family and friends that has nurtured their capacity to love and now surrounds and supports their relationship, shared history and memories, shared interests and convictions, shared laughter and tears, shared plans and dreams. We are grateful too for the differences that they bring to their life together—differences in family background, in personality, in talent, and in vocational aim. By what they have in common, by what makes each of them unique, and by the inspiration of your unfailing love, enable them to assume the responsibilities of marriage and experience its joys as loving and faithful partners—eager to share, slow to anger, quick to forgive, willing to sacrifice, and ready to grow together. May they prove to be people of their words. May the commitments they now make be experienced not as a burden but as a blessing. May they look back on this day's promise as a time when they did their very best. So help them, God, through Jesus Christ our Lord and the power of the Holy Spirit. Amen.

C. Eric Mount Jr.

Gracious God, giver of good gifts, keeper of promises, faithful lover of your people, and true friend, enable [*names*] to be good givers to one another, to be faithful keepers of their promises to each other, to be ardent lovers of each other, and to be the best friends anyone could have. Help them to love with the steadfastness that weathers the hard times and the imagination that adds sparkle to the good times. Inspire them to build a relationship that brings out the best in both of them and the uniqueness in each of them. Grace their home with such warmth and affection that loved ones will thrive there, friends will be comfortable there, and strangers will find a welcome there. Lead them to use their talents and abilities to reach beyond themselves to the communities in which they love and to others who need their help. Remind us of all the obligations that we assume by being here today. Since [*names*] wanted us here to share the beginning of their marriage, make us willing always to support them with our love and encouragement. Since we were part of the past that brought them together, make us part of a future that keeps them together. Bless each marriage, family, and friendship here represented, that we may cherish our loved ones, savor our time together, and so live that we not only find joy in each other's company but also find room for those others who need our love; through Jesus Christ, who embodied your undying love and invites us to pray: Our Father . . .

C. Eric Mount Jr.

Father's Day

Our gracious and wonderfully creating and creative God, we gaze into the face of a baby and are awed by your handiwork. We gaze into the face of your creation in stunning landscapes, in the heavens above, and in the moral law within and are awed by your handiwork. O God, as Nicodemus came to you in the night to find you, we come in the dark night of our souls to seek your light. In the darkness, we offer to you the burdens of our hearts: the secret fears, the toxic shame, the compulsion to puff up, and the desire to manipulate. We come to you in the night, O God, because we know that you are light and that you are love. We come to meet you because you have promised that if we seek you out, if we try to follow Jesus, and if we are open to the direction of your Holy Spirit, we will be born from above and become new people.

We offer over to you this day the prayers of our hearts: the joys, the sorrows, the sadness, and the hopes, trusting that you will enfold all of these into your healing care.

On this Father's Day we especially thank you for the gift of our fathers, whether we know them or whether they are strangers to us, whether they are no longer with us in this life or whether we are planning to spend time with them this afternoon. We thank you for their strength. We thank you for their weakness. We thank you for their love. We will never forget them.

O God, you know the concerns of the world. You know the broken places where your creation has been spoiled by war, violence, hunger, and want. We lift up these places to you, trusting that through us and through your people everywhere peace will be found, justice will be done, and your freedom will be known. We pray these prayers and all those left unspoken in our hearts in the name of the One who came among us to set us free, Jesus Christ our Lord and Savior, who taught us to pray together the common prayer, saying, Our Father . . .

Mark Smutny

Divorce

Make us sensitive, O God, to those whose marriages have failed, and show us how to support them as they go through the trauma of separation and divorce. But keep us from ever accepting such failures easily or treating the marriage bond casually. Hold before us the ideal that Christ held before his disciples, and grant us by your grace loving relationships in our marriages that reflect the love you have lavished on us. Amen.

Mark H. Landfried

Death

God of compassion, be with us when sorrow comes. Put your arms of love around us to hold us close, and underneath us to hold us up; through Jesus Christ our Lord.

Mark H. Landfried

Eternal God, God of our father and our mothers—our God—we come before you today not in sorrow and despair, but in joy and confidence. We come affirming our faith and confidence in your promises, as well as our blessed assurance that you are our refuge and our strength, a very present help in time of trouble.

We are witnesses of your loving kindness to your people throughout history, and of your presence with us now—in this sad hour. You are with us in every circumstance of life—in the joys of family celebrations and in the tragedy of death. Be with us now, O God, as you have promised you will be.

We thank you, eternal God, for life and for death. Especially today we thank you for the life of [*name*], whose faithful devotion was reflected in so many ways—in the love and devotion that he/she gave to his/her family, to many friends, to this church and this community, and to the world that you created and for which you made us responsible. We are so grateful, O God, for life.

We are also grateful to you for death. This is not easy to say at the death of someone we loved, but it is nonetheless true that as we praise you in life, we continue to praise you in death. We are grateful that [*name*]'s life was filled with accomplishments: with many friends, a loving family, a church and a community to which he gave devoted service. May your grace and your presence be with all those who loved him/her and who will miss him/her the most. Especially we pray for [*names of family members*] and for all who gather for worship today to remember, to support, to comfort each other.

Grant us all faith and hope—hope in the one who by death has conquered death and by life has promised life to others. Help us all, we pray, to live as those who believe and trust in the communion of saints, the forgiveness of sins, and the resurrection to life everlasting.

May we in faith and hope give back to you the life that was in love given to us, for we believe that in death—as in life—we are in your safekeeping. In our sorrow, make us strong to commit ourselves and those we love to your never failing care. In our perplexity, may we trust you where we do not understand, knowing that you, in the manner of a loving father, are always with us. In our sadness, make our memories grateful, as in sure and steadfast hope we commit ourselves and those we love to you.

Through Jesus Christ our Lord, who taught us to pray together: Our Father . . .

John T. Ames

Good Lord, we hurt today not only because of who we have lost but also because of what we have lost the chance to do or undo. If we had realized more, appreciated more, understood more, supported more, shared more, said more, loved more, our grief would not be taken away, but it might be easier to take. Take away our guilt by the power of your forgiving love, so that our selfish preoccupations may not blight our thanksgiving for the life you gave us and the loves we have yet to live; through Jesus Christ our Lord. Amen.

C. Eric Mount Jr.

God, in life and in death we belong to you. You know our names when we are in our mothers' wombs. You walk with us, sometimes in very obvious ways and sometimes in ways we do not notice, all throughout our days. And when we die you receive us. Having already prepared a place for us, you hold us in your everlasting arms.

This has been a week of difficult decisions, deep grief, terrible violence. And it has been a week where your presence has been palpable, your care revealed in the faces and bodies of others, your provision made known in ways we would never have anticipated.

The mystery of evil and suffering surround us. The mystery of faith and hope and love and grace surround us too. We ask for your comforting presence for all who grieve—in our own community and around the world. We pray for your healing in body, mind, and spirit. Sometimes your healing includes death, and we ask your tender care for those nearing the end of this life and for all who walk with them in this time.

No matter what the circumstances, no matter what the emotions, we remember the incredible truth that we are your children, and so we bring our prayers to you, praying with confidence as your children, and praying as Jesus taught his disciples, saying, Our Creator [or begin with the traditional "Our Father"] . . .

Ann J. Deibert

Serious Injury and Illness

When the world of our daily existence is suddenly turned upside down, O God, and suffering has come to us in a way we had never imagined possible, remind us that even such experiences as these can be a strengthening gift of your grace. In your mercy let them bring into our lives a deeper faith, a more genuine compassion, and a stronger witness to the suffering love of Christ, who leads us through the darkness to the dawning of a new day. It is in his name and in his love that we pray. Amen.

Mark H. Landfried

Gracious God, we give thanks for your abundant goodness to us. We know that you have promised to be with us through the valley of the shadow of death. We are in agony now because of the horrible accident that has happened to your child, [*name*].

We give thanks for all who are caring for her/him—for their skill and expertise, their compassion and concern, their understanding and affection. Grant them wisdom and insight, and guide their minds and hands so that they might be instruments of healing. O Lord our God, shower upon [*name*] the strength of your spirit and help her/him to live. Grant to her/him the awareness of your presence, calling her/him to new health and energy.

And grant to us, who wait around her/his bed, the comfort of your love that will never separate us from your son, Jesus Christ, who died and rose again that we might live. In his name, we pray. Amen.

John M. Mulder

Aging and Retirement

Lord, I am still not sure what I want to do. Give me indicators—some show of fleece for my lack of discernment. I suppose I can make a go of staying at my position. No one is forcing me to retire. And I can make a go of leaving and begin the search for new directions. Work on, or make retirement a chosen sabbatical—a time to develop other gifts: reading, writing, my mystical bent, and hobbies, whatever? I need a nudge for this before storming over the top to attempt the next position.

Why do I vacillate? I feel like Polonius, the acceptor of other people's opinions. Where is my spine? My decisive powers? My leadership ability? At least I know there is a plan

> That you will not leave my soul in Sheol,
> That providence involves a revealing,
> That prayer brings peace and purpose,
> That doors will open as well as shut; shut as well as open.
> Light my way, and show me that you have always been the Way.
> This your bewildered servant asks today.
> Be not far from me. Amen.

Robert D. Young

O God, I stand at the edge of retirement and don't know what is ahead. I am going from what I know to what is undiscovered territory. Is the allusion to death or to life? If I must acknowledge some measure to my days, what will be as significant as my work has been? And how can I avoid the false significance of keeping busy as a motor exercise, a false piety?

> And yet you have taught me, O God
> That the future is in your hands;

137

>   That you are continuing to do a new thing;
>   That I must trust in you with all my heart and lean not on my own understanding;
>   That I must forget what lies behind and reach forth to what lies ahead;
>   That I have circled the mountain long enough;
>   That I can rise, and start out again.

Take me into this uncertain territory, Lord. Show me how to play and how to work, how to live by faith and how to be energetic with good works—and show me where the line of demarcation is.

Bless you, Lord, for all your benefits. Your praise will continually be on my lips. When it isn't, send me a sharp rebuke until I realize again my good fortune in being one of your covenant people. Amen.

Robert D. Young

Lord, my times are in your hands. You know the circumstances of my beginning, the opportunities for growth, the experiences in schools and subsequent work. You know the times I've met opportunity head on and when I failed to rise to a challenge. All my ways are in your knowing, and all my times are in your hands.

So what now, Lord, at three score and ten? What is my calling when I've retired from a calling? Do you only call the young at some consecration campfire? Are you only the God of "productive years," when energy is high and memory keen? Or are you the God of all times who sets the burning bush in unusual locations? I wait to see what sign will mark the way.

You have said that there is a time to build and a time to tear down, a time to plant and a time to reap, a time to spend energy in a profligate way, and a time to rest and to be still and know. But what is called for when summer turns to autumn? A new rhythm of venturing and relaxing, or a pulling in of all investments—a summing up, as it were?

O Lord, you know. You know the skills you've given and the rich texture of experience you've woven, together with my desires and the gifts that now have mellowed. You know my times and the measure of my days. If it be your will, excite me with a call from some new horizon. I wait upon you; my soul waits more than those who wait to be entertained.

Be not far from me, Lord. Let me see the bush as a treasure in a field, and help me to discover it and turn toward it and give everything to possess it. I look for a challenge from you that's a gauntlet with a gift in it—the gift of a renewed joy in following Jesus, the gift of being on the road with him even yet. Amen.

Robert D. Young

A Prayer with an Elderly Church Member

Eternal and ever loving God, we give you thanks for this day and each day that you entrust to us. We give special thanks in this hour for your child, [*name*]. He/she has given so generously to your church and this community, and through his/her many deeds of charity and compassion, he/she has touched the lives of hundreds. Grant to him/her a renewed sense of your presence so that he/she might have the comfort of knowing that he/she belongs to you—body and soul, in life and in death. Sustain us with your Spirit so that we might walk in your light on the path you have set before us. This we ask in the name of Jesus Christ, who taught us to pray, saying, Our Father . . .

John M. Mulder

Graduation

Eternal God—God of our fathers and mothers, and our God—your power and your majesty and your love are revealed by the world around us and by the beauty that is within us. Your praises are sung by the prophets and poets of Israel, by sages and swamis of India, by the wise philosophers of Asia, and you are known to many of us through Jesus Christ, whom we call Lord.

Women and men of goodwill in every land acknowledge that you created the world and pronounced it good. We thank you for the wise order of our universe that is made known to us by science, and for the beauty of your creation that we know by art.

We thank you for memory, which enables us to build on the experiences of the past, and for imagination, which admits us to a wider world than we would otherwise know.

We thank you for our families with whom we live day by day, and with whom we share intimacies and secrets, with whom we make great plans and little plots, with whom we share the tragedies and the exhilaration of life. Keep us close as paths divide, and make our memories precious.

We pray, eternal God, for this school. We pray that helpful tasks may be done here, that students may continue to be filled with the joy of learning and that teachers may be sensitive to the high responsibility that is theirs.

We pray for the generation of which these graduates are members. Give them purpose and a sense of direction. Make them peacemakers in a world that yearns for peace. Give them a passion for the protection of the world itself. Make them sensitive to the worth and dignity of every other person. Help them to be radical where radical solutions are needed and conservative where old ways and values are still useful.

Guide each of them as they pursue the goals and ambitions and dreams that are the prerogative of youth. Guide them as they seek and find places of importance and fulfillment in your world. And guide each of us as we attempt to contribute to the fulfillment of the ancient dream of the prophet—

that the earth may be filled with the glory of God, as the waters cover the sea. Amen.

John T. Ames

Wondrous God, whose name we take in vain when we merely use it to decorate our ceremonies, we still risk praying at times like this not only because our forebears set a precedent but because these turning points heighten both our sense of celebration and our sense of sorrow. Something in us wants to rejoice in the possession of what can never be taken away, and something else in us needs to mourn the passage of what can never be repeated. In a way we are eager to get on with the future, but in another way we fear the future's threats and feel the pull of the tried and the secure more than the lure of the unknown and the new. We need to be graced with the faith that can at once look backward in gratitude and help us to find new meaning in a tradition that is both a legacy and a challenge. Enable us to experience now in a new dimension the satisfaction of what we have accomplished together, the warmth of what we have come to mean to each other, and the hope that insists on making places of arrival into points of departure. For today and tomorrow, so help us, God. Amen.

C. Eric Mount Jr.

Leader: Gracious Spirit, provider of life's best possibilities and lure toward life's highest fulfillment, even the unpracticed in prayer can muster the faith to call this day a blessed event. In our meeting here, memories of your goodness follow us, communicators of your love surround us, and promises of your faithfulness go before us. Putting your gifts ahead of our attainments, we are grateful for all who have furthered the development of this college that we now claim as our own,

People: And for all who helped our development as the people whom this college now claims as its own;

Leader: For a place on earth that we can always call home,

People: And for a circle of people that we will always call family;

Leader: For a point on the globe where we could get our bearings,

People: And for an island of civility where we could air our differences;

Leader: For venerable traditions that stay alive here,

People: And for bold dreams that come to birth here;

Leader: For the freedom that enabled growth,

People: And for the freedom that entails responsibility;

Leader: For broadened capacity to enjoy,

People: And for sharpened capacity to evaluate;

Leader: For moments of accomplishment that satisfied us,

People: And for seasons of discontent that energized us.

Leader: Eternal God, even as the contemplation of today moves us to count our blessings, the contemplation of tomorrow prompts us to voice our petitions. We confess that more than educational credentials will be required if we are to weather the future, much less ameliorate it. We pray for the social acumen that attends to the health of vital institutions,

People: And for the social awareness that attends to the voices of discounted people;

Leader: For care that the pursuit of happiness be an equal opportunity,

People: And for concern that the pursuit of justice be our common cause;

Leader: For public peace that far surpasses temporary truces in our new world disorder

People: And for private peace that far surpasses our educated attempts at creating inner calm;

Leader: For recovery of a nation, "one" and "indivisible,"

People: And for rededication to "liberty and justice for all";

Leader: For the spirit of openness that sees value in diversity,

People: And for the sense of vocation that finds meaning in labor;

Leader: For the vision to think globally,

People: And for the determination to act locally;

Leader: For the courage of faith,

People: And for the patience of hope.

All: So help us, God. Amen.

C. Eric Mount Jr.

Leader: Eternal God, to whose glory this college was founded and in whose service a great company of our forerunners here has labored, even on a day set aside to recognize each other's accomplishments, we acknowledge that we are not self-made people. Others have labored, and we have entered into their labors. Others have sacrificed, and we have been the beneficiaries. Others have dreamed, and we have been drawn into the orbit of their dreams.

People: We give thanks.

Leader: For the help that sometimes saw us through, sometimes bailed us out, and sometimes shook us up,

People: We give thanks.

Leader: For the growth that sometimes surprised us, sometimes pained us, and always stretched us,

People: We are grateful.

Leader: For the sharing that moved us to relationships beyond our roles, created common bonds in the midst of common endeavors, and turned coexistence into community,

People: We are grateful.

Leader: For the vision that has exceeded what we had previously imagined, included more than we can comfortably take in, and encompassed more than our unaided eyes could have perceived,

People: We offer our gratitude.

Leader: For a college to call our own and for a future that calls us to make the nourishment we have received here a movable feast,

People: We offer our gratitude.

Leader: O God, we are privileged people, but we are still in need, and we inhabit a needy world that sees our privilege as more than it can afford. From being deaf to cries of need and distress,

People: Save us, we pray.

Leader: From being blinded by ambition, success, or bias,

People: Deliver us, we pray.

Leader: That we should use the power of our positions to avoid questioning the systems, institutions, and organizations within which we function,

People: God forbid.

Leader: That we may rise beyond job and career to vocation,

People: Good God, inspire us.

Leader: That we may care as much for moral excellence as for intellectual or technological excellence,

People: Good God, inspire us.

Leader: For yours is the power, the wisdom, and the love to enable us.

People: Amen.

C. Eric Mount Jr.

All: Gracious God, whose goodness has made the past worth remembering, the present worth savoring, and the future worth anticipating, we rejoice today in innumerable blessings that we have often taken for granted instead of recognized as given.

Leader: For a world where détente can turn into dialogue and where formidable walls can come tumbling down,

People: We are grateful.

Leader: For a time of heightened awareness of the earth's creeping endangerments and humanity's blind prejudices,

People: We are grateful.

Leader: For the tradition of learning that we have inherited and for the experience that we have shared,

People: We acknowledge our indebtedness.

Leader: For a place where hard questions were posed and easy answers were challenged,

People: We acknowledge our indebtedness.

Leader: For a time to claim greater freedom and to assume greater responsibility,

People: We voice our gratitude.

Leader: For accomplishments that empowered us and mistakes that matured us,

People: We voice our gratitude.

Leader: For a community where others listened to us and cared about us,

People: We give thanks.

Leader: For the love that supported us in coming here and for the friendships that will accompany us in leaving here,

People: We give thanks.

All: O God, whose light can guide us and whose power can enable us, educate us to live as people devoted to knowing and doing what is good and right and true and beautiful.

Leader: With the humility to remember the help that brought us to today and the vision to discern the ways that will take us through tomorrow,

People: Endue us, we pray.

Leader: With the dedication to turn careers into vocations and the commitment to turn relationships into covenants,

People: Imbue us, we pray.

Leader: With the compassion that feels the hurt of others and the justice that addresses the needs of others,

People: Inspire us, we pray.

Leader: With the awareness that will enlarge the horizons of our concern and the integrity that will set the limits to our compromises,

People: Invest us, we pray.

Leader: With the resolution to prevent nuclear winter and global warming and the determination to protect the welfare of the vulnerable and to redress wrongs to the mistreated,

People: Embolden us, O God.

Leader: With faith to know an idol by its feet of clay and hope to reject cynicism for its surrender to inaction,

People: Enthuse us, O God.

Leader: With the courage to face life's trouble and pain without considering ourselves singled out for suffering, and the perspective to regard life's privileges as responsibilities instead of proofs of our superiority,

People: Endow us, O God.

Leader: With gratitude to appreciate each of life's precious gifts and graceful moments, and with wisdom to recognize how much we have yet to learn,

People: Infuse us, O God.

Leader: To you, O God, be the honor and the praise.

People: Amen.

C. Eric Mount Jr.

Gracious and holy God, who creates us in the image of holiness and gives us the promise of abundant life, we thank you for the gifts of growth and maturity. In your grace you bless us with the hope of goodness and the potential of well-being, and we pray that these blessings will be lights unto our path as we travel the challenging road of life.

We thank you for the milestone of graduation, and we thank you for blessing received to this point. We thank you for love enjoyed, for values given in your Spirit and cherished by those that surround our graduate, for faith, and hope, and the support of family, friends, and community. We thank you for the promise you instill at inception and for the inheritance of faith that makes that promise real.

Inhabit the graduates' hearts, O God, so that they may gain the confidence of one who knows not loneliness. Let your Spirit reside within their soul, O God, that they may be assured no trial is so great it will not end, no obstacle so overwhelming it cannot be conquered, no pain so intense it cannot be comforted. Influence their vision, O God, that they may see beyond what is to behold the beauty of what, through your grace, can be.

Lord, be with them. Guide their dreams, their thoughts, and their actions, that each may be a tribute to you and to those who love them. Keep them in the inheritance of faith, which so many have worked hard to provide, and help them continue to grow in your way. In the name of Jesus we pray. Amen.

Curtis A. Kearns Jr.

Saying Goodbye

Thank you, God, for those moments when good memories of days past come flooding into our minds even as we are saying our goodbyes and looking forward to new experiences in days ahead. May those memories be fixed solidly within us and remain as a source of joy to be treasured and nurtured, that the old will not be lost when the excitement of the new is at hand. Through Jesus Christ our Lord we pray. Amen.

Mark H. Landfried

New Friendships

One of our greatest blessings of life, O God, has been the gift of good friends who share with us the joys and the sorrows of life, its laughter and its tears; who know the times when words of comfort and assurance and guidance are profoundly helpful while knowing also the times when simple acts of loving support are enough. Help us to learn these same lessons, we pray, that we will be good friends to others as others have been good friends to us. And keep us always open for the building of new friendships, not to weaken the old but to share in an ever expanding circle the riches of your never ending love; through Jesus Christ our Lord. Amen.

Mark H. Landfried

Prayers for the Natural World

Grant us today, O God, a new look at your world and a new appreciation of all its wonders. Lead us by your Spirit to a heightened awareness of both creation and Creator, that we may be good stewards of your good earth; through Jesus Christ our Lord. Amen.

Mark H. Landfried

We thank you, O God, for the amazing ways in which the world of your creation is woven together into the beautiful fabric that it is. Show us how to be those who care for your world and bring your shalom of wholeness to it; through Christ our Lord, who walked on this earth and shared its beauty with us. Amen.

Mark H. Landfried

All around us, O God, are the evidences of your creative power and the reminder of how all things essential for life on earth have been given to us. So keep us, we pray, from moving blindly through our days, from failing to pay attention to the lessons these gifts have to teach us, from failing to witness to others the source of the gifts, and from failing to thank you for them. Forgive us, and use us as you will, in the name and for the sake of Jesus Christ our Lord. Amen.

Mark H. Landfried

Loneliness

Dear God, the loneliness that has so suddenly come into our lives has been hard to bear and seems impossible to overcome. We turn to you in this hour of need to claim your promise that in your mercy you will always be with us and will always care for us, that you will be our constant companion and our dearest friend. Embrace us in your love, we pray, and, as hard as it seems now, start us on the road back to life as you show us how to reach out to others in their loneliness as you reach out to us in ours; through Jesus Christ our Lord. Amen.

Mark H. Landfried

Jesus, you must have been very lonely when, as you faced death, your friends deserted you. I believe you can understand the terrible ache of loneliness that gnaws within me now. I know that there are people who care about me, but that knowledge does not relieve my pain. I ask for the peace that the world cannot give or take away. I ask too that you open my spiritual eyes so that I may see the lonely ache in other lives. Please empower me to reach out to them with empathy and love and the assurance that your promises are trustworthy, that you are with us always, and that comfort, strength, and love are ours for the taking. In the name of the only giver of true peace, we pray. Amen.

Sarah Enos Brown

Peace

God, we thank you for those who put their lives on the line in the search for peace with justice. May hardened attitudes be broken down and wounded souls healed, that your peace may come and your will be done; through Jesus Christ our Lord. Amen.

Mark H. Landfried

Make us to be those, O God, who, living in your image and following in your way, become your agents for breaking the chain of violence in our world. So fill us with your love that the darkness of hate may be driven out by the light of your life as we have known it through the love of Jesus Christ our Lord. Amen.

Mark H. Landfried

Surprising God
Within the seasons of our lives
We come to this season
Asking that you awaken our hearts
To the prophet Isaiah's dream
That one day there would be healing of earth
In which lions and lambs would become friends
    The child and serpent play peacefully together
That which is torn asunder be made whole
    And within this season, Holy God,
Awaken us from the slumber of indifference
Wash us in the gentle mist of your love
Grant us courage to beat our swords into plowshares
Guide us to the ways of your peace

In which, through which
A sister's sorrow is comforted
A brother's wounds are healed
Family relationships are not described by "domestic violence"
Great and Holy God
Of love born in simple places
Create within us a new longing for simplicity
Desire to live in harmony with all creation
Open our ears to your voice in the marketplace world
Direct our footsteps to your ways of justice and righteousness

Liberate us from our self-centeredness
    That we may find reborn in our lives

Your promise to keep hope alive
    And within that promise
May we lift up our voices with sages old and prophets new
    To celebrate your advent in each new moment of life
        When your way becomes our way
        Through him who is your season with us
        Christ Jesus. Amen.

Raymond Hearn

O Lord our God,
    on this day set aside for the purpose
    we pray your blessing on the peacemakers:

    Where there is illness,
        give kindness to those who bring healing.
    Where there is anguish of soul,
        give tender strength to those who console.
    Where grief is fresh,
        give strength to those who comfort.
    Where there is stress in our homes,
        give confidence to those who bridge differences.
    Where there is tension in our town,
        give voice to those of fair intention.
    Where there is division in our state,
        give words to those who see a greater vision.
    Where there is bickering in our nation's capital,
        give courage to those of character.
    Where civil wars fester and rage,

give tenacity to those who value another's clan.
Where tyrants reign,
　　give conviction to those who speak truth.
Where there is conflict among the nations,
　　give discernment to those who seek accord.
Where life and homes are shattered by flood and by earthquake,
　　give stamina to those who bring relief.

　　And, O Lord God,
　　　　where your church struggles to find itself
　　　　give us a vision of the Prince of Peace,
　　　　that we might aid in the answer
　　　　to those other prayers we make.
　　We pray in the name of Jesus Christ. Amen.

James S. Lowry

About the Contributors

*R*obert W. Abrams has been a pastor, missionary in India, staff to the Synod of the Trinity and to the Global Ministry Unit of the General Assembly. He now lives in Louisville, Kentucky.

John T. Ames, a native of Hattiesburg, Mississippi, served several pastorates in Maryland, New Jersey, and Kentucky before becoming minister of First Presbyterian Church of East Hampton, New York, where he currently serves.

Gwen L. Bronson grew up in the Christian Reformed Church, spent most of her adult life as a Roman Catholic, and is now Presbyterian. She is an elder in the PC(USA) and is currently attending Louisville Presbyterian Seminary.

Sarah Enos Brown was born and raised in Clifton Forge, Virginia, and received degrees from the College of William and Mary, the University of Louisville, and Case Western Reserve University. She is married to a Presbyterian minister, and recently retired after twenty-nine years of teaching.

Thomas W. Currie III is a native of Texas and has served two churches in that state, most recently First Presbyterian Church of Kerrville. He was recently called to serve as dean of the Union Seminary-Presbyterian School of Christian Education campus in Charlotte, North Carolina.

Ann J. Deibert is a pastor at Central Presbyterian Church in Louisville, Kentucky.

Bob Haseltine grew up in Santa Fe, New Mexico, and obtained his Master of Divinity degree at Louisville Presbyterian Seminary. He and his wife as co-pastors in a four-church parish in rural Kansas.

Raymond Hearn is a retired Presbyterian minister for whom ministry was a second career after thirteen years in public education. He has served churches in Iowa, Wyoming, Colorado, Kansas, and Texas.

Curtis A. Kearns Jr. is an ordained Presbyterian minister who serves as director of the National Ministries Division for the PC(USA) in Louisville,

Kentucky. He has a rich history of involvement with the church at all levels, in both elected and professional roles.

Mark H. Landfried is honorably retired from the PC(USA). He has served as a pastor, synod and presbytery staff member, and was director of stewardship training for the General Assembly Support Agency.

James S. Lowry is a native of Great Falls, South Carolina, and has served as pastor in Presbyterian churches in Alabama, Florida, South Carolina, North Carolina, and Tennessee. He was most recently interim pastor of the Government Street Presbyterian Church in Mobile, Alabama, and is the author of *Prayers for the Lord's Day: Hope for the Exiles.*

Philip Lloyd-Sidle is an ordained United Methodist minister currently serving at James Lees Memorial Presbyterian Church in Louisville, Kentucky. He has pastored congregations in Uruguay and the United States and has done some writing for the Worldwide Ministries Division and for Curriculum Development of the Presbyterian Church (U.S.A.).

Annie Jacobs McClure is an ordained Presbyterian minister. Annie is presently director of events and author relations at Presbyterian Publishing Corporation in Louisville, Kentucky.

Ann Marie Montgomery is copastor with her husband, David, at First Presbyterian Church in Murray, Kentucky. She is also director of lay pastor and lay leadership training for Western Kentucky Presbytery.

C. Eric Mount Jr. is Rodes Professor of Religion at Centre College, where he has taught since 1966. He has served the college at various times as dean of students, vice president, chaplain, and director of Centre in Strasbourg, France an international studies program. He is the author of several books, most recently *Covenant Community and the Common Good.*

John M. Mulder is president and professor of historical theology at Louisville Presbyterian Theological Seminary. He is the author or editor of several books, including *Vital Signs: The Promise of Mainstream Protestantism,* coauthored with Milton J. Coalter and Louis Weeks.

Robert Nagy is associate pastor of Goodyear Heights Presbyterian Church in Akron, Ohio.

Amy Schacht is pastor of Laurel Presbyterian Church, a spouse, a mother of two preschoolers, and a Doctor of Ministry student.

Donna Schaper is senior pastor at Coral Gables Congregational Church in Florida and has extensive experience as an interfaith liturgist and educator in Morocco, China, South Africa, Hungary, and France. She is author of several books, including *Altar Calls* and *Keeping Sabbath.*

Mark Smutny has served Presbyterian congregations in Ohio and New York, and is currently copastor of Pasadena Presbyterian Church in California, along with his wife, Barbara Anderson.

N. Graham Standish is pastor of Calvin Presbyterian Church in Zelienople, Pennsylvania, and is a teacher, retreat leader, and spiritual director. He is the author of *Forming Faith in a Hurricane*, *Paradoxes for Living*, and *Discovering the Narrow Path*.

Mary Marple Thies is a wife and mother, and serves the church as copastor of First Presbyterian Church in Stamford, Connecticut.

Susan R. Tomlinson has been an elementary school teacher, a short-term missionary teacher in Africa, and an activities director in a long-term care facility. She answered God's called to ordained ministry in 1990. She attended Louisville Presbyterian Theological Seminary, receiving her Master of Divinity degree in 1993. After her ordination in the fall of 1993 she was installed as pastor of the Limestone and Allen Grove Presbyterian Churches in West Virginia, where she still ministers.

Thomas Vandergriff has served as a pastor in South Carolina and as director of church marketing for the Presbyterian Publishing Corporation. He is currently pastor of Fourth Presbyterian Church in Louisville, Kentucky.

Louis B. Weeks is president and professor of historical theology at Union Theological Seminary-Presbyterian School of Christian Education in Richmond, Virginia. He has also served pastorates in North Carolina and Kentucky, and is the author or coauthor of several books, including *Vital Signs: The Promise of Mainstream Protestantism*, coauthored with Milton J. Coalter and John M. Mulder.

G. Todd Williams is a native of Spencer, Indiana, and now resides in the Houston, Texas, area. He is a pastor in the Christian Church (Disciples of Christ). He holds a Master of Divinity degree from Louisville Presbyterian Seminary.

Robert D. Young recently completed a thirty-two-year pastorate at Westminster Presbyterian Church in West Chester, Pennsylvania. He is the author of three books: *Encounter with World Religions, Religious Imagination,* and *Be Brief about It.* He and his wife run a hospitality program for clergy, where the emphasis is on homiletics.